The Footpath Way
In North Gloucestershire

THE FOOTPATH WAY
IN NORTH GLOUCESTERSHIRE

ALGERNON GISSING

First published 1924
This edition 2009
Reprinted 2019

The History Press
97 St George's Place, Cheltenham,
Gloucestershire, GL50 3QB
www.thehistorypress.co.uk

British Library Cataloguing in Publication Data.
A catalogue record for this book is available from the British Library.

ISBN 978 0 7524 4903 6

Typesetting and origination by The History Press
Printed in Great Britain by TJ International Ltd, Padsrow, Cornwall.

CONTENTS

PUBLISHER'S NOTE

First published in 1924, the views expressed herein are sometimes far removed from today's thinking, but often they remain curiously relevant. Gissing laments the lack of appreciation that many villagers had for their surroundings, blaming poor education, and depicts a changing Gloucestershire where traditional communities are starting to fragment. However, as he concludes when comparing the scenes to Wordsworth's descriptions of them, there is also much that has remained. Today's readers will recognise and appreciate Gissing's portrayal of Gloucestershire's countryside and wildlife, the impressive views from the top of the hills and the peaceful orchards in the vales.

The original work was titled *The Footpath Way in Gloucestershire*, even though it focuses on the area surrounding Willersey and Saintbury. For this reason 'North' was added to give a more accurate reflection of the content.

Although not a facsimile, the book has been sympathetically designed to mirror the original layout. The addition of an absorbing Foreword from Katie Jarvis and a stunning colour section add a unique aspect to this new edition. We are grateful to the following contributors: Graham Martin, Emily Locke, Regina Knut, Stuart Herbert, Nick Kaye, Chris Price and Alan Pilbeam.

FOREWORD

If you were to go strolling in the beauty of the North Cotswolds, perhaps seeking the rare pasque flower or examining the ruined spectres of villas once inhabited by great Roman visionaries, then I'd recommend you take along a friend of mine: a sensitive, appreciative companion, wise in the ways of the countryside, gifted in the art of conversation. The fact that the words he will speak are echoes from the 1920s; the fact that he now lies buried under the earth he once trod, is neither here nor there; for this erudite recorder of rural ways lives on through the book he wrote: *The Footpath Way in Gloucestershire*. May I introduce to you Mr Algernon Gissing.

Under normal circumstances, I'd begrudge you robbing me of even a moment of his time. But this reprinting of his elegant tome allows me to be magnanimous; to share him. For he is, indeed, the most delightful friend, writing at a fascinating period in rural history.

The date is 1924. Only six years previously, the wounded, shell-shocked men of the First World War had staggered back from the trenches to discover all they had fought for was changing before their very eyes. Indeed, the great Laurie Lee himself wrote of witnessing the closing chapters of a thousand years of history: 'It was the end of a semi-feudal life,' he recognised.

Perhaps this accounts for the tone of Gissing's observations. There is a yearning within these pages; an attempt to capture the sights he sees as if he knows he's reaching for something as ephemeral as a dandelion seed about to be borne away on a breeze: 'From the first celandine and chiffchaff to the last red berry left by the stormcock and fieldfare'; the 'sweet plaint of the lapwing'; Cleeve Cloud bespangled with yellow tormentil and rock rose; 'the delicious autumn fragrance breathed by the surging south-west sweeping up from the Bristol Channel'.

Born in Wakefield, Yorkshire, brother of the noted late Victorian novelist George, Gissing was described by the Arts and Crafts architect

Norman Jewson as 'A cheerful, bustling little man, a prosperous solicitor'. He originally set out to become a famous novelist, like George, but his several novels languished unpraised and undistinguished. It was in later life, therefore, that he turned his hand to non-fiction and wrote his *Footpath Way*. It was a wise decision; one that allowed his talents to roam as freely as he over the Cotswold countryside. For Gissing takes the scenes he views and presses them, like wild flowers, within the pages of his book. He leads the reader throughout the area – Winchcombe, Condicote, Snowshill, Saintbury, Chipping Campden, Willersey (where he, himself lived at the time) – and, along the way, introduces them to some of the local characters, particularly the multi-talented William Smith: parish clerk, sexton, musician, bell-ringer, road-mender and (most importantly of all) an Everyman of the Gloucestershire countryside who allows Gissing to glimpse into the rural soul.

But don't expect this to be a walking book: it's far more than that. For as with real walks, Gissing allows his mind to wander as he ambles over the wind-swept hills. Peppering his observations with quotes from such luminaries as Shelley and the Bard himself, he provides the reader with a commentary on all he sees from his own unique perspective. Perhaps unexpectedly, his concerns are not so very far from ours: labourers' cottages being turned into holiday homes; the disappearance of ancient orchards; rigid teaching leaving children no time to learn to appreciate nature and the great outdoors.

While reading this book will take your mind over pastures new, it's also prose in which you can lose yourself in an exquisite description of simple clouds; a rendition of the Caw-caw-caw; jack-jack-jack! of mischievous birds; the acrobatics of a squirrel; the wings of a peacock butterfly; the awe-inspiring quality of a cathedral-like barn; a tree with its moods and tempers. His portrayals of the countryside combine the microscope of a botanist with the paintbrush of an artist.

It's a book of sights, of feelings, of velvety touches, of tastes, of scents and of sounds: such as the church bells of old England: 'Then for New Year's morning they suddenly broke again into jubilant peals. Two or three owls were hooting off and on all the time, and just after midnight came the plaintive notes of a plover from a distant field, aroused, I suppose, by the bells. Amidst such a scene, and to such a unanimity of voices, how escape thoughts of the heart of England?'

Katie Jarvis

ONE

AUTUMN MISTS

All this morning I spent on Saintbury Hill. The white autumn mist through which I went up was dispersing at the top, and the warm sun came as a delightful caress after the chill fog which had clung to me below. Drops had kept pattering through the trees which overhang the hill road, but until I stepped into the sun I was not aware that I too had gathered as much moisture as everything else around me. I could not see myself properly as I was facing the sun, but if anybody had been coming the other way I fancy I should have presented an unusually dazzling appearance, at any rate for a minute or two. Every scrap of my rough tweed hat and rougher tweed clothes had got covered with the tiny glistening beads which were throwing their lovely gauze-work over all the herbage and turning the streamers and cradles of gossamer on brier and furze to matchless white lace. Unfortunately nobody saw me at that radiant moment except a green woodpecker and a jay. The one gave his broken autumn laugh merely, and the other cursed as is his wont. It was startling how greedily the envious sun stripped me of my splendour. Under that glow I went out in the faintest breath of steam, much thinner than that which was rising so delicately from the beautiful brown earth of a freshly sown field near by. My moisture was, of course, superficial merely, and no doubt my own warmth quickened the evaporation, for the grass, the bushes, and the cobwebs shone for a long time after. Those tiny particles of moisture huddled so closely together, yet without merging in one another, are very wonderful, and I suppose it is just that which gives a shining cloud its glory.

It was long since I had been on that hill, though familiar with it under every aspect for many years. This particular morning brought back old memories so vividly that out of sheer gratitude I begin at once to say what I can of this quiet corner of Gloucestershire, a task so long intended and, I am afraid, too long delayed. It is that part known of old as the hundred of Kiftsgate, lying between Cleeve Cloud and Stratford-on-Avon, and nowadays usually called the North Cotswolds. Whenever I come cycling back here from distant counties the peculiar graciousness of this bit of landscape always strikes me forcibly. It is not merely the smile of a familiar face. There is something in the soil, and in the natural features it has given rise to, which seems to touch the very heart of that poetic instinct which is the birthright of the whole English race, try as we will to smother it. Never, certainly, were such strenuous efforts made in this direction as during this new century. Even here, within two or three decades, one has had to witness greater changes in the life and landscape than had taken place in as many centuries before. But it is idle to complain.

> Nothing can be as it has been before.
> Better, so call it, only not the same.
> To take one beauty into our heart's core
> And keep it changeless—such our claim—
> So answered, nevermore.

It was on a somewhat similar morning, though still more wonderful, in that lovely autumn of 1887, that I first formed a real intimacy with this little parish of Saintbury. A good many years before that time I had made acquaintance with it, in common with the whole district, whilst scouring these hills during holidays of boyhood which had come to me like the realisation of wonderful dreams, To a bookish and impressionable boy, from north country industrial surroundings, it was nothing less than stepping into Elizabethan England, into the very orchards and headlands of red wheat of Master Shallow and his man Davy. The local language, the whole life and landscape, the very atmosphere itself, was in those days nothing but Shakespearean. But on looking back I can see it was that autumn morning in 1887 (what we ancients call the year of the first jubilee) that really crystallised for me this general impression. On that day in the sun above the autumn mist I first met and talked with the old clerk

of Saintbury, as the district for years affectionately called the late William
Smith. For he had then been parish clerk since 1834, and was to go on
till the reign of Edward VII. During those last twenty years of his life it
was my happiness to have constant intimate intercourse with him and his
gentle old wife, who died some years before her husband, and I can never
enough lament that I did not scrupulously Boswellise all that wealth of
local gossip I had from them. Much of it, of course, in one way or another
was woven into such Gloucestershire stories as I published years ago, but
a literal record in his own language of all the old clerk told me from his
own actual experience, as well as what he had from elders in his youth,
would have been of permanent social and historical value. Such as I can
rescue, however, will peep out here and there in the following pages.
In this chapter I merely wish to recall that day, and that first meeting, of
which this morning so vividly reminded me.

When I want a walk, especially in a mist, I prefer to go uphill. As I was
at that time living at the foot of the north west face of these welds, on
setting forth that morning I took the road leading to Willersey Bank, my
nearest point for ascending the steep slope. So dense was the mist that
I could not see across the road from my cottage gate. However, I knew
even then that if the mist is very dense and very white it will certainly
not be so much as 900ft thick. And this was the height I could command
on reaching the top of Willersey Bank. It did not prove to be quite half as
thick. On the road up the bank there is a gate on the left to a field path
leading to Saintbury Church, and although the mist did not seem there
to be in the least degree thinner, by some impulse I turned into the fields.
On reaching Saintbury Church, I came to a sight I have never forgotten.
Here I was just about 400ft above sea level, and here I had got to the limit
of the mist. All at once I felt a warmer and clearer atmosphere upon my
face. Looking up instinctively to the light, I saw a few feet above me the
outlines of the rolling vapour moving like steam before a sky of cloudless
blue, into which rose not only the cock on the church spire, but also the
head of one tall elm tree, vaunting its brilliant yellow curls in the sun.
The lower part of the tree was still in mist. So sudden and unexpected
was the change that it was difficult to reconcile that little detached cloud
of yellow leaves on its background of unfathomable blue with the world
I had for an hour been groping through, wet, chill and featureless. Two
rooks passing over called me to myself. Afraid that so beautiful a vision
must vanish, instead of crossing to the road as I had intended, I clambered
up the steep green pasture, behind the church, called Castle Bank, which
rises to the hilltop where are the green entrenchments of an ancient camp.

In a few minutes I too was in the sun, over the top of the mist, on a level with the cock on the steeple and the yellow head of the elm tree just before me. But how much more was there than that! The whole clear hilltop stretched away towards the dazzling sun, and after glancing that way I turned my back to it, and looked across that vast vale to the west ward, bounded only by the Malvern Hills and the Welsh mountains. The familiar vale had gone. Instead of it, under a speckless sky of profoundest blue, spread a whitish-grey sea as far as the eye could reach. The surface was not exactly level, but only irregular enough to give the impression of great billows, out of which here and there rose the yellow head of some tallest elm tree resembling a little lichened rock beaten by the waves. In the midst, about eight miles away, lay the top half of Bredon Hill, an island green in the sun, and at about the same distance beyond that the bold dark heights of the Malvern Hills.

Though I have mounted that hill for years since then, I have never again lighted upon a scene so impressive. The mists generally are fragmentary or local, interwoven with certain trees, gathering about a particular field or wood, or trailing along the bed of the River Avon, or the more distant Severn, and lovely as these are under an October sun they cannot, of course, have the startling effect of a total transformation of the whole landscape. Those who are familiar with the majestic effects of clouds and mist in a mountainous district might think these unromantic efforts of a champaign country very tame, but in my love of every bit of our natural British scenery I have long lost the folly of comparison. Every field and hill and stream is lovely in its own way, and unless we dwellers in the country can learn to see the individual beauty of our home surroundings, without the incessant craving for somewhere else, we can never bring content to a broken rural life. When the ground mist here is widespread it has not often so defined a surface above. It generally ends with a ragged, indeterminate top as it did today, and it does not always lie under a cloudless sky. But unless the cloudlessness has something to do with the levelling of the mist at our feet, I cannot say that I feel a sky without clouds to be at all desirable. For consummate beauty few skies in the year can approach the marvellous displays of cirrus which nearly always characterise the early autumn, and in this way at all events my sky of today far surpassed that expanse of what Wordsworth has called 'cerulean vacancy' of five-and-thirty years ago.

Otherwise the natural surroundings were not much changed. Several trees have disappeared, but plenty still remain. In the craze of those war years happily the green old camp was not ploughed up. In the wet and shining grass noisy rooks and jackdaws were still squabbling over the walnuts they had stolen from the trees below and carried up here to crack, and they might been the very birds I surprised at the same work so long ago. *Caw-caw-caw; jack-jack-jack!*—what an inseparable part these voices are of the autumn skies and landscape. Not all the glistening shingle overhead, the silvery grass and gossamer at our feet, the coral hips and haws under the mellowing trees, could ever be complete without them, even if blended with the drowsy rise and fall of the threshing machine far down in the hazy vale below.

One thing, however, was not to be repeated. Wander how I would over the old haunts I could not encounter the figure of the old clerk, or indeed any figure remotely suggesting the world to which he belonged. That at last has gone utterly, as completely broken up as the parish stocks which old William told me he himself had chopped up for firewood a few years before I met him. Still the memory was clear enough, and changed though the old clerk naturally became during his later years, no alteration could dim my vision of that autumn morning in 1887. When I was able to turn away from the vale prospect which had so impressed me on that occasion, I crossed the field on the hilltop to the old finger-post at the cross roads by Gunn's cottages. Then, keeping upwards, by the beech trees that mark the parish boundary, in about a hundred yards I came upon the interesting figure coming down.

In addition to being parish clerk and sexton, the old man was then parish road-mender as well. That lovely morning he was evidently having a look round to see what might have to be done at some other time. A delightful air of procrastination and leisure, characteristic of all this district, was even more pronounced in those days than it is now. In this respect human life takes but its part with the rest of nature. Nothing is strenuous. There is no haste. The very spirit of the land is enshrined in that phrase so constantly heard on every hand: 'It'll do for now.' Not a notion of finality could possibly enter into any form of effort that can ever be in hand. It occurred to me afterwards that all this had been very plainly depicted in that picturesque figure of the little old man I met coming down the hill. It is true he was then already nearing seventy, and in approaching him as a stranger he appeared to me very aged. But as we came together this impression was quickly lost. Though he leant on a stick, was lame and much bent, the clear blue eyes, apple cheeks, and shrewd humorous features which were raised to me gave not a hint of decrepitude. His age was 'as a lusty winter, frosty but kindly.' Seeing me stop, and obviously kindly disposed, with the universal rural courtesy of those days, the old man took the brim of his soft hat between finger and thumb as with a bow he answered my good morning. Then followed a conversation which I suppose touched me as forcibly as any I ever had in my life. Phrase, tone of voice, and subject were so ridiculously just what they ought to have been in that particular spot. Though he was clearly far above the level of the ordinary local intelligence, I soon learned that the old man had never had any eye for anything in his natural surroundings. The effect of that sea of mist beneath the sun was nothing more than 'a strange curious affair' making it 'uncommon damp and cold for those in the vale.' So I quickly left the aesthetic tack and made glorious headway with lammas wheat and last year's pippins. But as soon as it was polite to do so I got my curiosity satisfied as to the calling and position of a personality which had so engaged me. Here was immediately response enough, during that first hour I spent with the old clerk in accompanying him to his church and inspecting it in his company I laid the foundation of a familiar intercourse which was to be a source of delight for so many years afterwards I believe to both of us.

Out of the church naturally sprang many points of personal history. Here I learnt that the clerk was also a musician. He still played the violin and 'cello, and until loss of teeth had prevented his 'parting the sound,' as he put it, he was able to play a tune creditably upon any instrument, wind or string. From boyhood he had been regularly one of the ringers. But what threw immediately most light upon his life and character was the reference he made to a brass memorial plate in the wall at the north side of the east window, inside the church. This bears the following inscription: 'Within the Chancel of this Church are deposited the Remains of the Rev. John Theodosius Jones, B.A., who was Rector of this Parish from A.D. 1826 to 1851. He died the 8th day of April, 1851. Aged 65 years.'

It was with visible emotion that the old man pointed this out to me, and, as I was to find out afterwards, we seldom had half an hour's talk about anything without the name of Mr Jones being somehow brought into it. The clerk admitted he owed all his life to this kind-hearted rector. To my amazement, this bright and hale old man told me that he had suffered severely from epileptic fits in his boyhood and youth. He was the son of a waggoner at Newcomb, and lived at Gunn's, a cottage at the crossroads on the hilltop. No doubt Mr Jones saw promise in the afflicted boy, for after being two years in the parish the rector had him down daily to the rectory to educate the child with his own son. This was in 1828, when William Smith was eight years old. It appeared ultimately that the rector's purpose had been to prepare young Smith for the post of village schoolmaster, since his infirmity threatened to debar his making a living as a worker on a farm. But this intention had to be abandoned as the fits got worse, and when Smith's own maternal grandfather died in 1834, at the age of ninety-two, having been parish clerk of Saintbury for twenty-two years, the benevolent rector snatched another opportunity of establishing the poor boy in life by electing him to the vacant office. The canons require a parish clerk to be 'twenty years of age at the least,' but although William was then only fourteen, the rector and churchwardens, with the approbation of the bishop, overrode this regulation, and boy was at once installed in his grandfather's office, which he was to hold undisturbed for close upon seventy years to come.

There will be more to say of this office itself in a later chapter. I merely mention these few facts here as I learnt them on that day so vividly recalled to me, and they so materially heightened my interest in the new friend I had made. As we scrambled up the dark and narrow stone stairs to the belfry, each step worn perilously hollow with the feet of seven centuries, I remember I felt some uneasiness as to the recurrence of the fits, and begged my companion to remain below. But it was no use. He came on close behind. On reaching the first dim chamber, through which the bell ropes passed to the church below, and lit only by the oblique light coming between the slanting stone luffer boards, I stumbled over a vast accumulation of faggot wood quite a couple of feet deep over the whole floor.

'An awkward place to keep your firewood,' said I.

'To a certainty,' cried the old man with a hearty laugh. 'All brought here by the jackdaws.'

Yes, it was cleared out every few years, thrown down into the churchyard below, and made two or three cartloads. Whilst speaking I saw a perpendicular ladder rising to a small square hole in the floor about 20ft above us, and I began the ascent. Dissuasion was again useless, and I heard the old man following. But when I had clambered on to the joists to which the great grooved wheels of the six bells were attached, and from which the bells were suspended, I looked down the hole and with great earnestness protested I was satisfied, and was about to descend.

'I'll be with you straight,' was the only response. And really to my horror I saw the head of my lame old companion emerging at my feet. Soon his whole body was engaged in the acrobatic feat of climbing on to the framework from which I had to move to make room for him.

But seeing my real anxiety he reassured me by saying that he often came up here alone to oil the bells. Then as I could no longer help hinting at the fits, the old man gave me the astonishing news that he had never had a trace of one since he was twenty-three years of age, when he married, though until that time he would often be found prostrate in the road. This, of course, put me at ease, and I could enter into our examination of the bells in a very different frame of mind. Yes, in spite of that unpromising physical start in life, here was this intelligent old man still enjoying the best of health, with every faculty alert, at an age which many of his strong youthful companions had never even reached. And there can be little doubt that he himself was right in attributing so much of this, with such unbounded gratitude, to the benevolent Mr Jones. Education and intellectual interests that kind rector had given him, and through all my intercourse with the old clerk this was the main part of the debt that he invariably emphasised. Never once did I hear him refer to the material benefit of his office, though, of course, as I shall show later, this was much to him.

At last we safely descended, and relocked the church, for most country churches were locked in those days. In parting, it is needless to say, I promised both myself and my new friend a speedy renewal of intercourse, and as I made my way down through the wet and misty fields to Willersey I found that in spite of all my previous acquaintance with this particular district, my imagination had never been quite so strongly touched as by that secluded little village of Saintbury, rearing its spire and golden elm trees into that cloudless sun out of the mist, and holding forth a living hand to the earliest years of the century in the person of its picturesque old parish clerk.

TWO

ON THE SKYLINE

All along the face of these hills nestle such little villages, about a mile apart, which with the lands making up their parishes act as a link between the life of the vale and the lonely uplands. As I have said elsewhere of one of them, they lie like scrolls flung over the hillside in full face of the north-west wind and evening sun. Fine breezy wold on the top, with harebell and wild thyme on barrows and in the hollows of old camps; pasture, quarry and woodland on the steep, broken slope; and, at the foot, some hundreds of feet below, skirts of luxuriant corn land and orchard running from the grey villages out into the vale beyond. Saintbury is scarcely a typical one of these, for it is almost too small to be called a village. The two or three farms and cottages, the church and the rectory, the little school that used to be, are sprinkled so casually amongst the great elms as almost to lose the sense of association with one another. But it is just this that forms a great part of its charm. And in common with the rest it remains a precious relic of the placid home life of old England. Naturally some of these villages have managed to retain more of their old-world charm than others. For one thing, during the last twenty years or more the district has been discovered by the outside world, and this has brought about many changes. Too often is Wordsworth's *Admonition* brought to mind by various alterations to secluded cottages.

> Think what the home must be if it were thine,
> Even thine, though few thy wants! Roof, window, door,
> The very flowers are sacred to the poor,
> The roses to the porch which they entwine:
> Yea, all that now enchants thee, from the day
> On which it should be touched, would melt away.

Very much, accordingly, has thus melted under such a touch. But this, of course, was as nothing to the upheaval of the war, with its base legacy of council cottages and zinc huts. Indeed, it has sorrowfully to be admitted that not a few old cottages and farmhouses have been actually saved from collapse and disappearance by the 'harsh impiety' deprecated by Wordsworth. It does not seem to be realised how rapidly in many parts of the country our charming old villages are simply slipping away from us through the neglect or inability of the owners to repair. If by a sacrilegious touch two crumbling cottages are transformed into one little tasteful holiday residence, this is surely better than the loss of them altogether by collapse. Small peasant properties are highly desirable and all very well in theory, but unfortunately under present habits they certainly do not make for the preservation of what we love in our old rural life, or what has made that life the backbone of our nation. There has been now for many years a deliberate policy to exterminate our landed proprietors, but if anything like honesty and culture shall then be left, social historians of fifty years to come will recognise the debt our nation owed to them, and in deploring their loss will doubtless speculate by what formulas of communistic science their place may be taken, in order to recapture quickly old heroic virtues so wantonly destroyed, and which had been growing for centuries like oaks on an estate.

But although so small, the features and the life of Saintbury would afford texts, so to speak, for the study and illustration of all our rural social as well as natural history. Indeed, any parish can do that, but, of course, I have no such ambitious intention. I merely take this sweet spot as a starting point for recalling some of the inspiriting associations suggested by the whole of this fascinating landscape. The very name of Saintbury has its peculiar attraction, although its original meaning is not precisely what it seems. No parish can afford in itself outstanding examples of all the beauties of its neighbourhood. One will supply the best camp or tumulus, another a gem of a church, barn or manor house. Elsewhere you must go for a noble wood, park, or quarry. It can not be said that Saintbury is pre-eminent in any one of these things. If I were compelled to indulge in the foolish trick of comparison between the villages hereabouts, I should probably have to give the palm to Stanton, a wonderful spot lying a few miles along the hills towards Winchcomb, and which seems to fallen happily into safe and reverent hands. But here at any rate is dear little Saintbury, stretching from the old London highway on the hill top between Oxford and Worcester, down the slope towards the north, and out into the vale to touch the county of Worcester in the parishes of Bretforton and Honeybourne. The Gloucestershire parishes on either side of it are Willersey to the west and Weston Subedge to the east.

It is needless to say that in social life neighbouring villages are always intermixed, Friendships, relationships and intermarriages, as well as business dealings, occur between the various inhabitants. One may have an especially popular annual wake or other festival; another a favourite clergyman or particularly cordial Wesleyan chapel. A clever blacksmith, wheelwright or shoemaker may characterise certain villages. On the other hand there are, of course, rivalries and even animosities that tend to keep certain villages apart, and which have given rise to many a contemptuous epithet or libellous proverb. There can be nothing invidious in saying that, for two or three generations during the nineteenth century, the link between Saintbury and its neighbouring parishes lay mainly in its parish clerk. His musical abilities and social, even convivial, temperament brought him into great request for miles around. But from his earliest days he was no less needed on serious occasions. His beautiful old manuscript volumes of chants, anthems, and other sacred music, all copied by his own hand for parish use, show what the musical capacity of our smallest old villages was before the introduction of hymn books and a harmonium. The old clerk, of course, was never reconciled to the poor apology of a hymn book. In one of his latest letters to me in 1908, in writing of former days, he said: 'My old friends at Broadway who sang with me there when the new church was dedicated to Saint Michael are all dead. Fred Handy the shoemaker was the last. He was ninety.' This dedication took place in 1840, when the young clerk was just twenty years of age.

It is not this social life, however, that I was going to touch on here. My mind is still on that hill top in the sun, and I want to recapture a few of the vignettes left me from long wandering there, in addition to that first meeting with the old clerk. Both life and landscape along the uplands are so different from that of the luxuriant slope and vale as to afford every charm of variety within the radius of a very few miles. For one thing prehistoric earthworks up on the skyline always have a peculiar fascination, and all these hills are freely sprinkled with them. Life, too, in these 'unkid places,' as my old friend used to call them, bred a rough-and-tumble type of character in his opinion. Not that he was in the least given to any form of ignorant conceit, such as characterises the traditional parish clerk. The humility of a well-bred character was always his, and never by word or gesture did he affect to remove himself from the life to which he was born. He was just genially natural, as genuine as a block of stone out of the quarry; neither envious of those socially above him, nor supercilious towards companions of his own rank who had not been blessed with his early advantages. Still it generally did happen that if anybody we were speaking about had to be thought not quite the thing, it would be sure to turn out that he had come 'from Stow way,' or, like Clement Perks, was 'of the hill.' But this was only natural, and in keeping with the traditional reputation of the Cotswold hill folk. For centuries the whole of these uplands remained open sheepwalks – that tract of 'high wild hills and rough uneven ways' complained of by Shakespeare's Earl of Northumberland on his way to Berkeley Castle, and characterised, after inclosure, in a still severer way by the later traveller Cobbett. The latter, on leaving Cirencester, says: 'I came up hill into a country, apparently formerly a down or common, but now divided into large fields by stone walls. Anything so ugly I have never seen before.' Other epithets like 'cheerless,' 'miserable', 'abominable,' this good old traveller flings about in his usual manner as he travels towards Gloucester, but then his warm heart was looking out for crops, for food, warmth and clothing for an impoverished peasantry he loved so passionately, and he did not think this bit of country at that time went about the best way produce them. And, of course, he was in a vicious mood politically. But compensation awaited him. After ten miles, 'all of a sudden,' says he, 'I looked down from the top of a high hill into the vale of Gloucester. Never was there, surely, such a contrast in this world. This hill is called Burlip (Birdlip) Hill; it is much about a mile down it, and the descent so steep as to require the wheel of the chaise to be locked; so upon Sir Robert Wilson's principle of taking care of Number One, I got out and walked down.' Joy unutterable awaited the fretful traveller below. For the honour of that lovely country, and of old Cobbett too, I cannot help completing the quotation. 'All here is fine,' continues he. 'Fine farms; fine pastures; all inclosed fields; all divided by hedges; orchards a plenty; and I had scarcely seen one apple since I left Berkshire. Gloucester is a fine, clean, beautiful place; and which is of a vast deal more importance, the labourers' dwellings, as I came along, looked good, and the labourers themselves pretty well as to dress and healthiness. The girls at work in the fields (always my standard) are not in rags, with bits of shoes tied on their feet and rags tied round their ankles as they had in Wiltshire.'

Tender, chivalrous old soldier! Amongst too much vulgar abuse, always a true and gentle heart for girls and all womanhood. This old-fashioned, effeminate virtue may some day be found to have had a little value after all, to women themselves no less than to men.

It is not to be denied, however, that several parts of the uplands will strike many travellers today as dreary. Some of us can see many beauties in the barest stone wall countries quite apart from their great historic interests, but so far as these Cotswolds are concerned, it is obvious they must have lost much of their old wild charm since they were divided into walled-in partitions and cultivated. Bits of the primeval wildness are still happily to be found here and there, from which one may judge what whole miles of it must formerly have been. Saintbury itself has not any of this left, except perhaps that dingle by the coppice, but in the adjoining parish of Weston Subedge there is a goodly part of Dover's Hill and the Linches still at large, so to speak, of which on account of its association with the old Cotswold games I shall say something in a subsequent page. Willersey, too, on the other side, has a fine open pasture and large camp, but this has now for some years got into the clutches of the Broadway Golf Club, so is lost to most of the interesting wildlife that used to haunt it. What I may call the southern apex of Saintbury parish, for it narrows down to a sharp point between these two parishes close to the Oxford highway already mentioned, embraces merely a level ploughed field or two, the greatest attraction of which used to be the peewits and kestrel usually to be found there. But, needless to say, there are fine breezy views of the hill landscape around, particularly down Tilbury Hollow, a little wooded crease running north-east towards the grey old wool town of Chipping Campden, a couple of miles away.

Still, to anybody who loves to glance into the very source of things, these bare uplands always offer romantic interest in their abundant traces of prehistoric times. All our history begins here. The old walls and quarries are full of fossils, if you want to go back so far as that. But I was thinking particularly of the old camps and burial places; the flint and stone implements which the ploughed fields have supplied, and still supply, so plentifully; the British, Roman or earlier roads and trackways which traverse the lonely wolds. One of these last forms the very boundary of Saintbury parish on the east – the old Buckle Street, which, when it ceases to be the long straight Bidford, Honeybourne and Weston highway, mounts the hill fields here as a delightfully wild track, hugging the deep wood of Weston Park on one side, going due south, and taking you away by Broadway Hill towards Snowshill, the Guitings, and all that beautiful country above Winchcomb on the way to Bourton-on-the-Water, Northleach and Cirencester. I believe most of it is still represented by a beaten road, but here and there it becomes merely an imaginary line, literally as the crow flies, over walls, ploughed fields, and impassable quagmires. Nonetheless, it is well worth the attempt to follow it, for whether you satisfy yourself or no as to the visible existence of the track, you will certainly get what seem to me the most characteristic peeps into the real spirit of these hills. And this, after all, is the main object.

There is no attempt in these pages to go into much antiquarian detail. Every parish must gather that for itself, and, for those who care for their landscape, much delight will be found in ransacking the vast stores of local material collected in archaeological and natural history publications, as well as the documents mouldering away in their parish coffers. It seems that the earliest mention of this street goes so far back as the year 709. In describing boundaries in a Saxon charter of this date, Buggilde Street is mentioned three times as being on the Stanton Hills. In the year 967, it is called Bucgan Street, and the authorities seem to identify it as either part of the old Riknild Street itself or as a continuation of it. At Bourton-on-the-Water it joins the great Fosse Way. The rough bit of it in Saintbury parish is still always called Buckle Street Lane. Many old burial places are about this ancient trackway all the way across these hills, the last being known as Wagborough, in the parish of Upper Slaughter. But for the ordinary observer these facts are quite useless if they do not suggest something picturesque to the mind. At any rate, so far as any educational value is to lie in the study of local scenery, it is plain that this must be imbued with a touch of imaginative pleasure in addition to any merely historical or scientific curiosity. So far as my own observation goes, the absence of this is the main cause of the so-called nature study in elementary schools having such pitiful results. The very simplest of children love the imaginative side of things, particularly of those things associated with the open air, and it seems deplorable that so precious a faculty should not only expire for want of encouragement, but should be so often even actively crushed by mechanical and unsympathetic teaching. But this is by the way.

Though every month, week and day of the year offers its various charms here as elsewhere, I think the golden days of autumn seem to bring out most distinctly that peculiar velvety softness of tone which especially characterises these rolling uplands as a whole. But of course you can only really know and love a landscape from familiarity with it in detail through all seasons. From the first celandine and chiffchaff to the last red berry left by the stormcock and fieldfare, the pageant of the year affords numberless delights which mysteriously blend to stir up that singular emotion binding us to the landscape and so familiar to the open-air soul. A single flower or bird really seen and realised in its characteristic setting has a marvellous power of flashing upon our 'inward eye' in such a manner as to enshrine for ever all details of the scene, and a great part of the enjoyment as well, with which it is associated. This is perhaps especially so with regard to this bare hill top. For my eye is now strictly towards the wild, towards those geometrical stone walls which Cobbett found so horrible. All view of that great luxuriant vale is cut off. To be sure nearly all here is cultivated – barley, mangels, sainfoin, or clover – and the outlines get more and more defaced with larch plantations, instead of those glorious clouds of native beech; but never mind, Our later life, unfortunately, cannot be passed in the wilderness. There is compensation, too, in the lonely grey farm buildings which cultivation has called up, dotted here and there as if they had actually grown from the soil, as well as in the tiny grey villages nestling in some crease or cup from which a rill has issued, Since they worked with Nature and not against her, our forebears throughout the land instinctively found the aptest, hence the most beautiful, use of local material in building their homesteads. But really no dwellings in the land seem quite so appropriate to their locality as these of the Cotswold stone, We call them grey, and so they are; but there are many qualities of grey. This one, for instance, is quite different from the sheep-like grey of Westmorland, the sombre gritstone grey or the silver limestone grey of Yorkshire. Here, it is a golden grey, which seems to absorb the very autumn sunshine, and is shown to perfection when you chance to see a late peacock butterfly with flat open wings printed on a wall in the sun. The stone roofs are invariably of a duller, darker grey, which, however, only heightens the general effect. There is a positive solemnity about these humble buildings, blended with the mysteriously velvety texture of the rolling landscape that I have referred to, which arouses something very much akin to religious emotion in the beholder. Indeed, you come upon a great barn occasionally, with its porch and little slits of windows, which inspires all the awe of a cathedral. These glorious buildings, with their dusky light inside and great complex rafters dimly revealed overhead, coupled with straw and sacks of liquid grain, and all the subtle scents about a homestead, go straight to some primeval instinct, surely sacred, which I cannot attempt to analyse. The very sources of human life itself seem centred here, and all the wild eccentricities of a material civilisation become mere delirium.

Yet all these beautiful relics of past centuries are but things of today when compared with the old trackways and burial places of primeval tribes, Even Roman villas are modern in comparison. These earliest memorials can only be associated with the very flowers and herbage that have so tenderly enfolded them, and the winds and plovers that still keep up for them their gentle wail. Down on the slope such bits of the old tracks as remain unused as modern roads have become entangled in the hedgerows which enclose them, buried under stacks of traveller's joy, brier roses, and blackberries, but up here they are open, about five-and-twenty yards wide sometimes between stone walls, under the shelter of which a white or black thorn has got rooted, an odd ash sapling, or a stray rose bush. The whole surface in such parts is covered with deep rank grass, on which the traffic of an occasional farm cart or team of horses leaves scarcely any impression. This grass, too, takes a golden hue in autumn, and does not allow many flowers on its domain. Some hardy cowslips will vaunt over it in the spring, but its real associates are the later harebell, pale lilac scabious, yarrow, large-rayed purple knapweed, and those two noble thistles, the musk, or nodding, and the woolly-headed one, *nutans* and *eriophorus* of botanists. To sit under one of these last, often as much as 5ft high and branched in all directions, in the sun of a late September or an October day, when the goldfinches are beginning to come up from the gardens and orchards down below, and to watch these radiant little gems rifling the great woolly heads and scattering the down on the gentlest of breezes, is one of those sights which make you want to live on herbs and spend all your days out on the wild heath, Still, one can be thankful for small mercies, and happily a great deal can be seen in a couple of hours with eyes sharpened to 'the keen edge of seldom pleasure.' As a result of the noble efforts of our bird protectors, there is not the old risk in speaking of the whereabouts of our precious birds. The effect on the multiplication of goldfinches, for instance, is perhaps one of the most obvious of these good results. In many parts, of late years, the goldfinches may be called plentiful. Their sweet plaintive call and their blithesome twittering greet you on every hand, and they seem anything but shy birds. I have positively lain under the branches of one of these noble thistles without being heeded at all by the three or four goldfinches at work upon it. And I know an exposed garden, open to a village highway, and a few yards from a railroad of constant noisy traffic, where these birds have built for several years in an acacia tree, and very beautiful it is, not only to hear their sweet notes incessantly, and to see them picking about the trees, but also to watch them bathing during the hot summer days in the dish put regularly for the birds' drinking. But the curse of village gardens are the cats. No protective laws can restrain these prowling ruffians, and every cat in a village becomes an inveterate watcher and hunter of birds. The toll they take is enormous. Nobody can be a lover of cats and birds as well. You must take sides.

For rare plants, however, there is no protection, and one hesitates to talk much about them, With the exception of the common bracken and male fern this is not a ferny country, and I know of three distinct lanes from which the very last root of hart's-tongue on which I had an eye has disappeared. Of course, such a fern cannot be called rare, but hereabouts in a wild state it is, and one resents its actual extirpation at the hands some foolish collector who probably let it die from drought a week or two after it was transplanted, and who could as easily have got a root from a friend's garden with a better chance of establishing it. So-called botany lessons become another danger, so that things like the pasque flower, the bee and other uncommon orchises, and what not, would seem better left to waste their sweetness on the desert air rather than risk their extermination by hinting at the places where they grow. Perhaps the one in greatest danger is the pasque flower, that beautiful anemone which does not lurk in woods and which waits until the last spring snow has really gone, and the cold Easter winds are at any rate softened by the May sun, before raising its purple head above the turf of the exposed sheep pastures which alone it loves. It has not too many resting places in the land, and it is gregarious in its habits, so that it is easily assailed in bulk when discovered. In this locality I know of several attacks upon it with basket and trowel, out of sheer love unfortunately, so how is the assault to be averted? Gathering flowers is, of course, one of the purest and most instinctive enjoyments of the country from childhood upwards, and it is not even desirable that we should all cultivate that somewhat morbid excess of sensibility that would see sentient life in flowers as in animals, and shrink from taking it, Still, since the law cannot easily protect them, it is to some such sense, I suppose, that we must appeal in defence of our rarities, and I beg anybody who goes to hunt for the pasque flower with trowel and basket, or even with a simple pocket knife, to think of them as living gems passionately attached to their native home, and, before digging a single root, to ponder first and very earnestly the most exquisite expression of the sense I have referred to which English literature affords. It comes from the soul of Walter Savage Landor, and long as the quotation is I must give it all, since it is not likely to be known to any but professed literary students. After asking when had he ever denied his hand to a plant buffeted by wind and rain, which had needed protection, he exclaims:

'Twere most ungrateful; for sweet scents
Are the swift vehicles of still sweeter thoughts,
And nurse and pillow the dull memory
That would let drop without them her best stores.
They bring me tales of youth and tones of love,
And 'tis and ever was my wish and way
To let all flowers live freely, and all die
(Whene'er their Genius bids their souls depart)
Among their kindred in their native place.
I never pluck the rose; the violet's head
Hath shaken with my breath upon its bank
And not reproach'd me; the ever-sacred cup
Of the pure lily hath between my hands
Felt safe, unsoil'd, nor lost one grain of gold.

Let us all, then, at least extend these tender scruples to every rare flower we encounter on our way. A pressed and labelled specimen, except for study in some established collection, is a wretched substitute for the precious living plant which we can have a delightful ramble to look at. If we take only the flower without the root we have in all likelihood prevented its seeding, and so multiplying itself several-fold the following year. It is much the same as shooting a rare bird which might otherwise have nested with us. Happily, everybody begins to condemn that atrocity. There are, after all, hundreds of lovely flowers that we call common, of which we may bring home a handful for pleasure or study without any uneasy feeling that we are robbing a beautiful landscape of any of its interest or charm, and in all probability with the positive merit of discovering some fresh beauty that we had so long ignored before.

THREE

WHERE THE PASQUE FLOWER GROWS

In the old days, the word 'trespassing' never entered one's mind in wandering about these uplands. So long as you left gates closed or open as you found them, did not damage a wall or fence in getting over it, and otherwise behaved as a well-conditioned mortal, your presence, by farmer, keeper or shepherd, seemed to be welcomed rather than otherwise. Many a delightful interchange of experiences was naturally the result. But a different spirit seems to be creeping over the land now. Barbed wire is coming more and more into fashion; actual pathways are being blocked up; stiles are being made as far as possible insurmountable. Indeed, only a few days ago I was positively challenged as a trespasser on a beaten road which has undoubtedly been a public way for many a century, and which it is to be hoped will continue so for many a century to come. But as that particular case is under the consideration of the local council it is hardly necessary to enter the fray. I merely mention this to warn readers that my airy rambling comes mainly by way of happy reminiscence, and to let them know that where I gathered rosebuds and found unalloyed inspiration and enjoyment, they may very possibly be met with insult and be ordered off the ground. To adopt the words of the ordnance maps, the representation of a path in these pages is no evidence of the existence of a right of way. So, with this proviso I must have a look at the pasque flower at home after all.

The spot where I know it best is one of those wild bits of pasture which I have mentioned as remaining to show us what large tracts of these wolds must formerly have been. It is sprinkled with gorse, self-sown thorn and elder, some of the thorn trees being very old, with weirdly twisted trunks, and with heads fantastically carved by the wind. There used to be one in particular, bending with eagerly outstretched hands to the east, 'as if craving alms of the sun,' to adopt the beautiful expression applied to similar trees in *Wuthering Heights*, but I missed my old friend when last I wandered there.

These old thorn trees are a delightful feature of many of the wild parts of these hills. I don't remember to have noticed it just here, but many of them in various localities are freely tasselled with mistletoe. It does not seem to grow to any great size on the thorn, or often to bear berries, so far as I have observed, but you will frequently see good tufts with branches radiating a foot or two all round, of a golden green, standing out very prominently from the purple twigs and the dark red haws of the leafless winter thorn trees. The pasque flower, however, seems to avoid these trees, and indeed shelter of every kind. It will only occupy the open pasture. Cowslips and the bright dog violet will nestle up to the very trunks of the thorns, if it is not one that sheep, colts and cattle have chosen for a rubbing post, in which case even the grass itself will be worn away, and the trunk some feet from the ground will be as smooth and nearly as hard as polished granite.

One seems to look with peculiar affection upon an old hawthorn tree, probably because he is so seldom allowed the full stature of his natural life. Even their very name is a badge of servitude. Because of their efficiency in fulfilling a particular office very useful to mankind, they are condemned to that use for ever, being unmercifully hacked and dismembered into merely artificial shape and proportions, to the loss of all their best physical and spiritual life, Perhaps this is why one rejoices to see those fortunate enough to have escaped their bondage. When you are allowed to see what they really can do, it seems hardly possible to exaggerate the wonder of their wild charm. To find this in full play you must follow the old track of Buckle Street some miles farther towards Bourton-on-the-Water. Surely nowhere can there be finer displays of the hawthorn in natural life than on those lonely uplands of Kineton and Eyford. There are whole acres there which can only be called hawthorn woods, for the trees far outweigh the rough pasture amongst them, which latter becomes simply a network of green glades and passages amidst a labyrinth of hawthorn. I am not greatly impressed by a mere mass of white blossom, except that it chances to come in with the sweet of the year, but in the endless variety of weird gesture and quaint contortion these trees afford inexhaustible charm through all the seasons. Not that charm was quite the word I wanted, unless we import into it also that added sense of occult suggestion which superstition gave it. I know of no tree that possesses this magic in quite so marked a degree as the old hawthorn. A grove of them is the very place for mystic or fairy rites. There is, of course, none of the dark solemnity of great forest trees that meet overhead; still less of the lifeless gloom of a fir or larch wood; but in all the elements of superstition, fancy or romance a wide stretch of upland thorn trees is not to be beaten.

Although Peter Quince lives in Athens, and arranged to meet his players 'at the duke's oak,' when they come together in the wood he has to exclaim: 'Here's a marvellous convenient place for our rehearsal. This green plot shall be our stage, this hawthorn-brake our tiring house.' Nothing, certainly, could be better. And our Shakespeare himself without doubt knew well these hawthorn-brakes of Cotswold, and had seen many a 'fallow greyhound' outrun up here besides that of Master Page. Even in the Forest of Arden, Rosalind has to complain that 'there's a man hangs odes upon hawthorns and elegies on brambles.' But this, she no doubt suspected, was that they should not be too high for herself to reach.

It seems to be mainly these gestures, and what I have ventured to call contortions, of the full-grown thorn tree that give much of the weirdness to its character. It becomes a positively elfish quality, and is not only seen as between tree and tree. Various antics appear in the same one. The tree has a common habit of throwing up several trunks from the same root, and as they grow older these lean away, intertwine or intersect, in a way suggesting all sorts of moods and tempers. By invoking a friendly wind, sometimes a recalcitrant member has stretched far enough to get blown down, and there, although shackled at the foot, he sprawls outwards on the turf at full length, on hands and knees as it were, seeming to flourish with renewed vigour in his partial deliverance from the family bondage. If the whole strength has from the first been put into one trunk, even this will frequently, at last, divide, and in extreme age, when rain and canker have eaten away the heart, the two or three slices of shell remaining will bend away under the weight of an increasing separate head, tottering on to the inevitable fall.

But I should be sorry to suggest the impression of struggle and decay from a glorious grove of hawthorn. Needless to say that is not the general effect at all. Still, if you feel anything about it beyond the mere pleasure of gathering may, or the fascinating lines of drawing, I do think the effect

is as highly suggestive as that of any trees that live. Downright tragedy is
not wanting. Most of us love ivy, I expect, but to see an old thorn tree in
the grip of an ivy tree almost as old, is as moving as the Laocoon. It can,
indeed, be likened to nothing else. The frightful coil of an ivy trunk 5 or
6in thick, which in return for support has pressed itself into the very skin
of the poor old hawthorn so as to be sometimes barely distinguishable
from it, is a harrowing sight. The triumph of the ivy, too, is abominably
exultant. It flourishes so outrageously that its victim is buried under a
whole stack of exquisitely green leaves, out of which two or three dead or
dying limbs are stretched forth in pathetic ghastliness, and perhaps one last
valorous and vigorous branch that has had strength to thrust itself far out
horizontally in the effort to escape the octopus tentacles is being slowly
and surely over taken by those beautiful little tender shoots embracing it
so lovingly to its death, The contest is too unequal.

Still, it is needless to point out the folly of taking moral or sentimental
sides in our observation of nature. It is certainly a temptation to some
of our best human tendencies, but it can be so easily carried to excess,
and all joy in natural associations would very rapidly be crushed under
a weight of morbid sensibility. The individual life itself is obviously not
of the importance we should like to attach to it. Nor are we to think
that death itself, under natural conditions, is what we call an evil or a
cruelty. The problem which puzzles some of us is how a prolonged and
harrowing death can so easily be inflicted in what is known to us as the
spirit of sport. This passion in mankind for mere killing is very strange, for
it is not really natural even to the lower animals. The purpose of killing
is usually for self-protection or to procure food. But our boasted love of
sport has long since very far outstript that. Even if it were an instinct in
man, instead of an elaborately cultivated vice, it must surely be seen by any
candid mind to be one contrary to the whole bent of human aspirations
and development, and one which has to be as rigorously rooted out as any
other far less brutal vice which all have agreed to conquer.

This has, however, carried me far away from my subject, which was
the very reverse of tragical. It was in the joys of the upland and thorn
brake that I was revelling, and amongst its other attractions lays the fact
that where the trees and bushes are thinnest, allowing of wide spaces
of smooth pasture, the pasque flower grows. This little treasure is one
of that lovely group of flowers classed under the buttercup family. The
Anemone pulsatilla of botanists, with its better-known white sister of the
woods, beloved of everybody, stands as one of the only two truly wild
representatives our country affords of a beautiful band of some seventy

species. Though they give us such a variety of exquisite colours, the whole family is entirely devoid of petals. As in our so-called Christmas rose, marsh marigold and other flowers, the anemones have enlarged the usually little insignificant cup called the calyx into floral sepals which in wonderful beauty out-vie many of the possessors of a legitimate bloom. The pulsatilla is by no means one of the loveliest of the band, but possibly because it is so rare, and because its native haunts are so exhilarating to the home wanderer, this flower inspires a peculiarly strong affection in those who find it. Evidently old Gerarde felt it so, by being moved as he said to give it the name of pasque, or Easter, flower, which has remained with it. But it is very seldom in flower by Easter nowadays. The March snowstorm frequently lingers on till April on these bleak uplands, and the pasque flower usually waits until it can vaunt in the May sun before rising its 6 or 7in above the elastic turf. And to know what it is, it must be seen in the sun. Under the clouds it remains almost closed, only showing its dull outer covering of silky hairs which clothe the outside of the blossom. But in the sun it fully expands, and the pale violet-purple colour has then a singular power of asserting itself amidst the green, more conspicuously than many an intrinsically fuller hue. Each stalk bears but one flower, large for the size of the plant, and about midway up the stalk is a frill of narrowly dissected leaves standing upright when the blossom is fully grown, but which had closed round the bent head of the bud. As the flower fades, the real leaves round the root, like uncurled parsley leaves, become more and more apparent, and get to their full growth when the coloured sepals fall and the central tuft of seeds which they have sheltered form their silky plume of feathers, so like and almost as big as that of the old man's beard. Lovely as the flower is itself, it is of course also associated with all sorts of lovely things in those spring days. Besides the flowers and trees, the sunny air is full of life and rippling with the song of skylarks. The cuckoo calls all round, and behind, somewhere, beating like the sacred heart of the universe, you almost feel rather than really hear the sweet pious notes of the blackbird. Of the wonders of the sky over that great expanse of downs, and the colours it imparts to the rolling landscape, it is hardly possible to speak, for it requires the art of the brush to convey even a hint of those impressive effects.

One evening, however, of a day I had spent up there I very well remember and must recall. It was towards the end of an especially warm and brilliant May. Between six and seven o'clock I was at last turning my face homewards for a walk of many miles, and was accompanied for some distance by a little willow wren whose nest was, I suppose, near. He sang continuously his sweetest of all songs as he came on, openly and fearlessly, from bush to bush just beside me. I mean he sang repeatedly rather than continuously, for, exquisite as it is, his song is short, just trilling, almost stumbling, so sweetly down the scale and it is done. But with only two or three seconds between he began again, and so on over and over again, until I passed to a large open field without bush of any kind. Having thus so tenderly led me off the premises, he came no farther. Sorry to part, I looked back almost due south, the evening sun behind me, and forgot my little bird in the startling beauty of the sky. There had been travelling showers around throughout the day, though I had had none, and the sky had been glorious with varied clouds on the profoundest blue, although the wind was south. Now as I looked there was a dark storm cloud creeping up over the green hill, right in face of the sun, and across it a magnificent rainbow over-arching the old camp. Cuckoos were calling, and the uproarious bleating of sheep and lambs came from a shearing at a farm a mile away. I strode forward and kept looking back at the threatening storm. But I got none of it. As the cloud advanced it parted, but the rainbow continued brilliant, and the arch enclosed in it, down to the green hill below, soon became a mysteriously sunny blue. This space was literally flanked on right and left by the deepest slate-coloured cloud, which was absolutely parted by the rainbow. As the blue sky spread, the rainbow became exquisitely thinner and fainter till it died altogether as I was getting to the brow of the hill. There the wooded slope and the wonderful vale under the sun drew me to other things as I came back to the luxuriance of these lower lands again.

FOUR

BELAS KNAP

The very atmosphere changes directly you pass that rim of the hills. It is the boundary line between two quite distinct countries. No doubt the eye plays a great part in producing this impression, but it is more than that. Every sense becomes aware of the immediate change. If you ascend this north-west slope at any point between Mickleton Hill and Birdlip, a few strides at the summit alter the whole tone of your reflections. That is one of the joys of living upon or under what the geologists call an escarpment. Even without a wide ground mist to work the illusion, you can easily imagine a great sea occupying that rich vale, washing up to the fine headlands and filling the coombs and inlets that diversify that beautiful front. But I have not quite done with those lonely rolling uplands.

These delightful and suggestive contrasts offer some compensation for the one great sad want of this district when compared to that lovely sister region into which it develops a few miles to the south. And some compensation, it must be confessed, is needed for the absence of those upland streams, the Churn, the Coin, the Leach and the Windrush. Nothing else in a landscape can quite take the place of what a north countryman would call its waters. Here there are literally none. Such little brooks as can gather together at all in the creases, or down below in the fields, are but magnified ditches, though they will manage sometimes to give you a sweet bit of babbling talk under the trees. Those beautiful little tributaries of the Thames are, however, within reach of a day's ride or ramble, so may contribute occasional delight if not actually available as daily food,

After glancing at the charm of water, it is almost ludicrous to plunge into the other extreme and say that the old burial places, or barrows, have a peculiar fascination for some of us. But they certainly have, and these are virtually confined to the open downs or the fields that have been enclosed from them. Many have been levelled by the plough, but I believe something like 200 are yet claimed to be in existence in the Cotswolds. The later barrows are round, and these are more numerous than the earlier ones of the Neolithic period, which are called long, on account of their more or less oval shape. One of the two principal ones in Gloucestershire is within our district, on the hills between Winchcomb and Cheltenham. Not only on account of their greater age are these more impressive than the merely round barrows. Their very form and structure make them vastly more imposing. Though called long they are, when unearthed, strictly of an elongated heart shape, the wider end being beautifully curved inwards at the entrance to the graves. The other of the two I have referred to is in the south-west part of the county at Uley, and it is really the more important. This one has obtained the local popular name of Hetty Pegler's Tump, and from its entrance has an actual passage to the chambers of the dead. But the one I am going to speak about is called Belas Knap, and I have not heard of any less dignified name having been given to it. Though pronounced with a short 'e', it has nothing to do with any heroine of the name of Bella. As may be readily supposed, the authorities are by no means agreed as to the origin of the word, and as I am very far from an authority I shall not venture to meddle with such a topic. But I must confess to being pedant enough to have taken Sir Thomas Browne's *Urn Burial* in my pocket more than once on a summer's day and passed some hours with him there beside the wild thyme in the sun. Never did the old physician's glorious periods roll more solemnly than in that drowsy hum of the bees and flies amongst the flowers on those violated graves. For it is not possible to rid one's mind quite of that sense of violation. I crave for the knowledge disclosed, but find it dearly bought at the cost of desecration. At least when we have stolen our knowledge, measured the skulls and sifted the last spadeful of ashes, it seems unpardonable at all events to leave these old works, whether of pride or piety, in such squalid disorder. One would have thought that mere gratitude for the contribution to the riddle of human life we had extracted would prompt the trifling return of clearing up at least the material disorder we had wrought in gaining it.

But there the old graves lie open, the covering earth and stones flung in confusion aside, just as the pick and shovel left them. The human remains found in the whole barrow consisted of no less than thirty-eight skeletons of both sexes and all ages. 'What time the Persons of these Ossuaries entered the famous Nations of the dead, and slept with Princes and Counsellors, might admit a wide solution. But who were the proprietaries of these bones, or what bodies these ashes made up, were a question above Antiquarism. Not to be resolved by Man, nor easily perhaps by Spirits, except we consult the Provincial Guardians or Tutelary Observators.' We of later date have presumably consulted these high authorities, for we do not hesitate to rush in with every imaginable detail where Sir Thomas feared even in faintest outline to tread. I should very much like to have seen the spot before it was first opened nearly sixty years ago. I can find no illustration or exact account of this original condition. The flowers that grow naturally on that upland turf are amongst the sweetest our flora affords, and they always seem to clothe with peculiar tenderness these prehistoric graves. It is to be presumed, therefore, that the spot presented merely an oval mound of green turf, standing nearly due north and south, considerably wider and higher towards the north end and tapering gradually southwards. The length given in the local archaeological society's publications is 197ft and the breadth 7ft at the widest part, diminishing merely to a rounded point. There must certainly have been rabbit holes in it, and amongst the grass would be cowslip, blue bird's-eye, harebell and wild thyme; yellow cistus and tormentil; fairy flax, blue milkwort, and mouse-ear hawkweed, with no doubt a gorse bush or two. But if one begins to think of these flowers, is it fair to leave any out? Several that have got footing now, owing to the broken surface, would certainly not have been there originally. But one may safely vouch further for yellow rattle, rosettes of dwarf thistle, burnet, scabious, and the big knapweed. Aye, and many more, even in those few yards of ground. How musical their very names are, and how full of fragrant breeze, sunlight and skylarks' song!

It was some account of the excavations, however, that I intended to give, and this, like the measurements already mentioned, I will take from the archaeological volumes. The measurements quoted are presumably those of the mound before it was touched, taken, I suppose, from the margin where the earth began to rise above the surrounding turf. About a yard, then, within this outer margin is a wall of slaty stone about 2ft high, except at the north end where it rises to 7ft and gradually curves inward so as to make a passage toward the centre. This terminates about 20ft from the outer margin at a massive slab, set vertically between two pillars like rude stone gate-posts, and with them supporting a still larger stone set horizontally, but there was no entrance. At the sides of the barrow are two smaller openings leading to chambers, and there is another at the south end.

A large flat stone lay exposed on the surface of the barrow near its south end, which on being removed was found to form the cover of a cist 6ft long, 2½ft wide, and 3-4ft from the surface of the mound. Its sides and one end were formed of large, rough, flat stones, the other end consisting of a semicircle of dry stone walling. This cell was filled with rubble, amongst which were found the remains of four human bodies, two male and two female, and with them were the bones and tusks of boars, a bone scoop, some fragments of sun-baked pottery and a few flints. Subsequently, an excavation was begun at the summit which came down upon the large stone previously mentioned as covering the false entrance. In clearing this, a small piece of Roman pottery bearing the mark of the lathe was found. On the stone was a lower massive jaw with no other bone, but immediately under the stone the remains of five children were discovered, ranging from one year to seven years of age, and with them was a very remarkable skull of a man without any other adult bones.

In the year after this excavation the exterior wall around the east side was explored. About the centre the wall was found to dip in, forming a passage about 2ft wide (it is nearly four) leading to a little chamber which was then fully excavated. It was formed of four large, flat, rough stones enclosing an area, somewhat square in shape, of about 5ft on each side. It would seem to have been roofed in the usual way by overlapping thin stones, which had given way, the superincumbent mass falling into the chamber, causing a depression which had been noticed on the surface of the barrow. In this chamber originally, squatting on flat stones around the walls, must have been placed twelve bodies which the falling of the roof had crushed flat. On the western side of the barrow was a chamber almost identical with this. It contained fourteen bodies, differing from those on the east side inasmuch as they were of all ages, whereas in the east chamber they were all of middle age. No pottery, flints or other remains were discovered.

A further investigation was made of the northern entrance referred to, but no cells or chambers were found, though there were appearances of the ground having been disturbed, and pieces of broken pottery of the Roman and Romano-British period were turned up. Nearly in the centre of the barrow, a little broken circle of stones was discovered, the soil around them being mixed with wood ashes. The diameter was about 7ft, but no remains of any kind were found near it. At the southern end of the barrow appeared an opening leading into a small chamber, which appeared to be perfect and untouched. Portions of a human skull, some teeth, and a deposit of animal bones, probably wild boar, were met with in working down to it. It was walled all round, covered with three large horizontal stones, each about 3ft sq., but it only contained pieces of broken stones.

As already stated, the human remains found in the whole barrow consisted of thirty-eight skeletons of both sexes and all ages. Though most of the skulls were crushed, the examination proved all of them, with one exception, to have been of the long-headed type. The exception was the skull found under the large stone referred to, which in every respect presented a marked contrast to the other skulls. It belonged to a well-developed round head. One of the explorers thought this skull suggested a secondary interment, but the other one thought this quite impossible, and considered it more probable that this skull and the remains of the five children represented rather prisoners of war from some distinct tribe immolated in honour of those to whom the barrow was raised.

Such is the account given by the archaeologists who directed the excavation of the barrow. Most of the remains discovered are now in the Cheltenham Museum, but all the other features of the barrow which are referred to remain on the hill top just above Honeybee Wood, which drops down to the little village of Charlton Abbots. To come suddenly upon what is called that false entrance at the northern end is really most impressive. To speak merely of a wall of slaty stone which gradually curves inwards gives but a very inadequate idea of the exquisite beauty of the stone and curve alike There are no marks of tooling, but the evenness of the outer surface is perfection, and the curve, rounding to the entrance, is faultlessly constructed in the Hogarth line of beauty, known to architects as 'ogee'. The stone used consists of those beautiful grey flakes with which the Cotswold houses are roofed, most of them barely ½in thick, and but a few inches long, laid horizontally one upon another to the height of 7ft. So at least it was when first opened, but it is now a foot or two lower owing to the action of weather and human feet in displacing the upper stones. They are built up without any kind of cement, but lie truly upon one another with little more room than will take a paper knife between. That beautiful bit of work alone shows an artistic instinct in those primitive ancestors of ours, which surely ought to have been respected. But we throw open their graves and leave the elements to obliterate at last all traces of their remembrance. In their simplicity they made a better bid for perpetuity than we do. As Sir Thomas says, 'In vain we hope to be known by open and visible Conservatories, when to be unknown was the means of their continuation, and obscurity their protection.' But these traces of art in them suggest 'a question above Antiquarism.' Why should high material development seem so inevitably to divorce us from the soul of beauty which pervades the natural universe? What made those rude Neolithic ancestors of ours, who were probably barely clothed, and had never heard of any sort of metal, hit on that beautiful ogee curve and see the exquisite grace of those thin layers of truly laid stone? It is no injustice to say that very few indeed of our twentieth-century war memorials can match the innate beauty and dignity of such a simple structure.

When completed and the bodies interred, I suppose the hole would be covered in with broken stones, and over them the stony soil of these uplands which is called stone brash. Even if it was left as a mere mound of broken stones alone, the elements would very soon crumble it and throw over its surface the turf and flowers I have spoken of. It is 3-4,000 years in any case since the barrow was erected, and how soon the rain, snow, and frost, the sunshine and the wind set about their beneficent work can be seen by watching an unused heap of roadside stone, which is almost buried in herbage the second year. Owing to our excavations and the disorder we have left, their work is harder now. The graves yawn open, and the great stones are tumbled down, so nature has thought it best to set about in a very resolute manner by planting trees and brambles and briers. Where any footing is possible, the little modest flowers have regained their hold, and have added wild strawberry and many beautiful mosses to their band, whilst crimson spires of the rose-bay willow-herb rise up 4-5ft over them. But, if left to themselves, the self-sown saplings will in a few years over-canopy the graves and be draped in the feathery plumes of traveller's joy, which is now seeking something to cling to. Already, some are far taller than a man, rise oak, ash, hazel, willow and thorn, whilst some bird has thoughtfully brought berries of a wayfaring tree to the spot, which, in addition to adorning already the mound with beautiful leaves, will soon return the bird's piety with a crop of fresh berries of their own. Of an additional hazel bush I must confess to having deprived the spot, for a year or two ago my eye fell upon a cracked nut barely covered with earth which was already rooted there and had shot up into two or three leaves, so I brought it away to my garden.

It is an impressive spot, and perhaps never more impressive than towards sunset on a still, mild, north-west day, such as you get most years between Martinmas and Christmas. Those bluish-grey ridges or great bars of cloud which show their white linings against pure blue space, out of which the travelling sunlight on the clear landscape has been so wonderful all the afternoon, grow heavier and closer ridged as their marvellous colour becomes deepened and intensified. Perhaps only one bright long slit will remain round the west sky with the bare head of Cleeve Cloud printed against it. But follow it on towards the north and there will lie the noble little range of the Malvern Hills, darkened to the profoundest damson blue. Though the sun orb is hidden or gone, the solemn clouds overhead will show, here and there, mysterious tinges of gold which will change to pink and then rapidly die away altogether to a lifeless grey. The peewits have been wailing over the fields, the fieldfares have left the hawthorn berries, and down in Honeybee Wood the owl is already hooting. That is the time to dream what you like of the Stone Age.

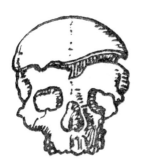

FIVE

WOLD VILLAGES

I t is not to be supposed that these 'high wild hills and rough uneven ways' are quite given up to camps and barrows, desolate farmhouses or isolated barns. Every few miles, generally in some little open hollow, an orange-coloured lane will lead you to a grey group of houses clustered about a church to form a village, and the cheerful cries and clean rosy cheeks of the children by no means suggest any sense of hardship in their lot. I do not refer to such beautiful spots as the two Guitings, for there the real southward valley has begun, and though typical Cotswold villages of the best kind, they are far too luxuriant in their green pastures and under their great trees to be taken as a sample of the real wold village. Snowshill, Cutsdean, Ford and Condicote are the best examples of what I mean. Here, the rolling open uplands are all around you, dotted with plantations or narrow strips of wood, mostly of larch unfortunately, and to come upon one of these little old-world communities of a sudden gives you a singular thrill of astonishment. They are such startling pictures. It is true they are surrounded for the most part by those geometrically enclosed barley and turnip fields which rather spoil their landscape pictorially, but in the villages themselves you forget all that. Here, everything suggests, at all events, not only real but beautiful life. If you talk with the inhabitants you may find, unhappily, that all things are not exactly what they seem, and that the free joy of the faces and voices of the children may get considerably dimmed after leaving school. How to bring to these villages some sense of their numberless blessings is by no means clear, but it is very obvious that mere improvement in economic conditions does very little, if anything, towards it. Many other remedies of increased social activities are being widely tried, but there are ample signs that the result from these also is far from what we require if the essential soul of country life is to be restored to its place as the mainspring of national sentiment.

It is a fallacy to suppose that country life should be stimulated from the same sources as that of the town. The two temperaments are and ought to be essentially different, as different as that of man and woman, and the more the rural mind is led to adopt the town attitude, the deeper will be the national loss. These would seem mere platitudes if all practice did not so consistently ignore the vital truths involved. Of course, it may be argued, as in the case of the sexes, that the two are now on the same plane, so that it becomes impossible, even undesirable, to differentiate. Surely it is nothing short of a calamity if this should ever prove really to be so. Something more, at all events, one would think might be done in youth to awaken the rustic mind to some sense of beauty, from which might spring as we know not only admiration, but very likely some spark of the other two poetical aspirations of 'hope and love' as well. Town and country alike would gain from them.

Recently, I had to get the key of a small Norman church in a remote village hereabouts, and in taking it back to the civil cottage woman who had lent it to me, I remarked on the beauty of the building, which indeed was obvious enough to any eye irrespective of archaeological curiosity But with a smile, almost of pity, she only said, 'I can see no beauty in it.' I talked for a few minutes, of course without effect, and as I went on I had to confess that my friend the old clerk of Saintbury, intelligent countryman as he was, would in strict honesty have had to make exactly the same blunt admission as this simpler countrywoman. Education, surely, ought to be able to do something towards remedying this. Yet I think there can be no cynicism in stating what is clear to everybody, that after fifty years of compulsory schooling, the mind of country people is farther removed from content, and therefore from the perception of any beauty about them than it ever was. Instruction, no doubt, of some sort they must have had, but it has evidently been of a kind 'which, though it gives no bliss, yet spoils for rest.'

Try how you will, in our present-day life it is hardly possible to escape these vexing social questions, though they sadly interfere with the calm enjoyment of what you came out to see. There is no lack of sympathy in saying this. It is pure nonsense to talk of the intolerable hardships of a farm labourer's life. That construction of it arises only from the distorted fancy of a sophisticated townsman. If urged by a countryman it can only be from love of mischief or the ramblings of a discontented mind. The man who has done his duty and has got on with his work tells you a very different story. He, from the time, mind you, when wages were from 7-11s a week and no free cottage, has brought up a large family, and has been able to take a farm. Mrs Sturge Gretton, in her work on the Cotswolds, was able to state a few years ago that 'two fine old men now living in Charlbury tell me that they married and were happy in the forties on 7s a week. Certainly they brought up their children well, and these children are all tradesmen or master workmen now.' This in the hungry forties even. Numberless later such instances could be afforded to show that it is all simply a matter of character, the very thing which our popular education seems to have done so little to develop. Yet with all his thrift and contentment, the successful countryman, as a rule, has not learned to see any beauty in his surroundings. That must be frankly admitted. Ask him to admire his beautiful old church, the grey stones of his lovely old homestead, or even the colours of his wife's flower garden, and he will probably say with a grim smile, 'You get ne'er a boiling off 'em.' Still he has never canted about his hard lot.

Now, it is hardly possible to believe that this was the attitude of mind of the folk who built the homes of these little grey villages. The very stones cry out in denial of it, Yet we know there is no labourer on the land now to whom the material daily life of those forefathers would not appear one long intolerable hardship. Nonetheless, there is abundant evidence that those so-called hard lives were full of jollity. Rough and rude, if you like, often even intolerably brutal, yet somehow or other all their extravagances fell into inimitable picturesqueness. Hard as it seems to reconcile, their piety also was a stern reality and no merely conventional gloss. I suppose it is beyond dispute that the puritanical spirit gave the first blow to this life of robust mirth, and that the destruction of the village community by the eighteenth-century enclosure acts finished it off. Ever since, the mere materialism of an industrial development has robbed country and town life alike of any pretence to imaginative influences.

The countryman of all people wants his heart back. Recreations of country folk, surely, should grow out of country life, as they all did originally. They should be as native to the soil as the flowers that established themselves on Belas Knap. Nearly all the simple inhabitants of these villages are strictly of the soil, direct descendants of the folk that established their faultless surroundings, and if by an understanding of their long past these descendants could recapture some sense of continuity with their ancestors, it does not seem improbable that they might begin to see some 'beauty in it,' and that from that small germ might develop a new measure of imagination consistent with the genius of their life and soil.

It is scarcely necessary to point out how this blank indifference to the beauty of their surroundings has already destroyed many of our villages, and in what rapidly increasing danger it places all the last crumbling treasures of our countryside. There is no vestige of local taste or reverence to stand in the way of destruction before the paltriest plea of utilitarian development. It is idle to talk of progress and the effect of education when we see daily the trend of things and the hopeless light that has to be put up for the graces of life and the protection of any threatened object of beauty or historical interest.

The widespread and ingrained indifference or even contempt for mere beauty is a thousand times more dangerous than any spasmodic outburst of popular rage, and, if I may again take the liberty of quoting Mrs Gretton, I fear on this account her reasoning is fallacious when she says: 'Endangered as the old house may think itself today by democratic feeling, it is really less in danger than at any previous time of its history. Bitter voices heard about the place now are as nothing compared with the bitterness which seethed dumbly out of sight of it a hundred years ago.' True enough, no doubt. But that old smothered bitterness was not poison at the root. It arose from a definite cause, from the anguish of cold, hunger and despair; from human souls frenzied under the stings of brutal injustice and quite intolerable wrongs. Read those old agrarian trials, if you can bear to do so, those old administrations of the poor laws, and then wonder that the whole constituted authority of the country did not go up in flames to heaven. The merest crumbs of just and human dealing, the smallest spark of instinctive sympathy, would at that time have averted all such frantic misery, as well as the bulk of what has since made our danger so much more deeply rooted, entrenched at the very source of our civilised life.

All this, then, out of those few grey stones of such a village as Snowshill, Cutsdean or Condicote, when all you long to do in gazing at them is to forget it, so as to lose no scrap of the blessing inherent in the mere picture. But how escape that old question Fra Lippo puts to us:

> Do you feel thankful, ay or no,
> For this fair town's face, yonder river's line,
> The mountain round it and the sky above,

> Much more the figures of man, woman, child,
> These are the frame to? What's it all about?
> To be passed over, despised? or dwelt upon,
> Wondered at?

The answer of those chiefly concerned is immediate. We see no wonder or beauty in it. And as for thanks, that sentiment naturally could not arise where you see nothing to be thankful for. Fra Lippo, we may remember, saw help for such insensibility even in his brush, and urged in defence of it:

> For, don't you mark? we're made so that we love
> First when we see them painted, things we have passed
> Perhaps a hundred times nor cared to see.
> And so they are better, painted – better to us,
> Which is the same thing: Art was given for that.
> God uses us to help each other so,
> Lending our minds out.

If this supposition of his is well founded, it is to be hoped that our best landscape painters may some day find patrons in the Education Committees of our County Councils, so that not only village schools, but village clubs and halls as well, may play a part in opening the minds and hearts of the parishioners to the charms of their own home life and landscape.

Words can do little for such scenes. Biographies, so to speak, might be attempted, for it is the only way, but not portraits. And even for an outline of its life every village would require a volume. Each parish should compile this for itself, and with a little efficient direction would soon find the greatest entertainment in doing so, for all country folk are not even yet so advanced as to be taken up with futile speculations upon the future of the world. They love, above all things, gossip of the past. There lies little Condicote, for instance, which for centuries has drawn its homely life from those lonely wolds. No doubt for mutual protection, as well as mere personal comfort, the inhabitants drew closely together from the first. I believe there is an explanation offered that such closely-knit villages, as distinguished from those that are loosely scattered, represent a Saxon settlement in a district from which the earlier natives had been entirely driven out. If so, this is one. The farmhouses with their golden-thatched ricks, the grey cottages and Norman church, cluster round a little plot which was no doubt originally a village green, but has now, unfortunately, become a vegetable allotment. Beside it was the spring of pure hill water for the use of all, over which the piety of the fourteenth-century gratefully erected a cross mounted on three steps, for the destruction of which down to the very socket no doubt puritanical frenzy was answerable as for so much else of the kind. Shaft and head were, however, restored about the middle of the last century. What the original head may have been, of course, can not be known now, but how beautiful these little village crosses were (and nearly all of them had one) can still be seen by the few old ones remaining fairly intact. The original steps at the foot of the Condicote cross at all events remain, worn hollow by generation after generation for centuries, who clambered about them in childhood and came to sit upon them in the evening sun of their old age. For this the stones were erected.

Several villages have, of late years, revived this pious custom by putting up crosses to the memory of those they lost in the recent war, but, incredible as it may appear, many of them have taken the precaution to enclose their structure in spiked iron rails with a locked gate. The effect and the suggestion may be imagined. To complete the picture, instead of the sweet green grass creeping up to the foot of these crosses, the ground about them is encased in a concrete pavement, not even stone, which may bid defiance for centuries even to a dandelion, Scarcely any better evidence could be afforded of the pass our village life has reached, or I would rather say has been supposed to have reached, for nobody need believe that the normal village population has sunk to such a depth as that. Those railings are nothing short of an insult to the village at large wherever they have been erected. If parents and schoolmaster have not inspired their children with a proper feeling towards so sacred a memorial, it is hardly necessary to say that whatever else they may have taught them is worse than useless. But we need not believe it. If those memorials were surrounded by an open patch of grass, and the little children, having been taught their meaning, were allowed to play around them, learning to jump first from the lowest step, then from the second, and at last from the third, nothing but very positive good from it could ever come to them. Their eyes would get unconsciously trained to a beautiful picture, instead of inured to a hideous monstrosity, and they would no more think of injuring such a memorial than they would the stone on their mother's grave.

With reference to the remote situation of Condicote in this formerly wild hill country, and the compact nature of it, it may be interesting before leaving to mention that the Norman church was dedicated to St Nicholas, not only the patron saint of scholars, but also of travellers and merchants. Hence, his aid was especially invoked for protection against robbers, to whose depredations this isolated little settlement might seem peculiarly exposed. By a facetious inversion of the situation we may recollect that the robbers themselves received in cant language the name of 'clerks of St Nicholas.' Oddly enough, Saintbury Church, too, is dedicated to St Nicholas, situated as it was beside that lonely old trackway of Buckle Street. And as the trade of thieving was never peculiar to any one age, it was interesting to hear from the old clerk that tradition of his own day associated the famous highwayman, Jimmy Hind, a kind of Dick Turpin, with the Saintbury roads and parish. A hedge alehouse, which formerly occupied the site of Gunn's cottages at the crossroads on the hill, where the clerk himself in childhood lived, was said to have been a retreat of Hind's.

It would be delightful enough to trace the story of all these little villages. Every one of them is included in the Conqueror's 'Domesday Book,' so of course goes very much farther back. No doubt almost from the foundation of the settlements until the middle of the eighteenth century the economic life of these communities with their open common lands was little altered. Nor would the sports and pastimes be for centuries. Coursing was, of course, always one of the favourite recreations along these hills, as Shakespeare well knew, but enclosure and cultivation put a stop to most of this as well as other games. It was the seventeenth year of George III (1777) that saw 'An Act for dividing and inclosing the Open and Common Fields and other Commonable Lands in the Parish of Condicote.' As elsewhere, that wrought a revolution in the social and economic life of the place. After the first inevitable upheaval, we know that a good deal of merriment survived or was recaptured. Harvest homes continued for quite another century as a regular feature of the Cotswolds. There were still fairs at Stow-on-the-Wold, only some three miles away. Even to this day the children can raise a bonfire to burn Guy Fawkes, at least I suppose so, for I know they can at Cutsdean as I saw the smouldering ashes of it there but a day or two ago.

Snowshill even still boasts its annual wake, but of these festivals I must not speak until I get down the hill to Willersey. Indeed, Snowshill, an almost-perfect hill village as it is, owing to its proximity to the brow of the hills, is more within reach of polite life, and so cannot retain quite so much of its primitive wold character. I remember seeing there, however, many years ago, oxen in use in the fields, a practice long since dead. A year or two ago certainly I saw a team of these magnificent animals at work in the neighbourhood of Northleach, but these no doubt had been introduced for the mere pleasure of the thing. Snaweshille, as it appears in the *Domesday Book*, perhaps shows some sign of having been more in the world by the fact of its Enclosure Act going seventeen years farther back than that of Condicote. It was in 1760, the first year of George III, that was passed 'An Act for dividing and inclosing certain Common Fields and Common Meadows and a Common Hill called Snows Hill, lying within the Manor of Snows Hill,' etc. But, after all, mere priority of enclosure gives little evidence of situation, for as we shall see presently, the open fields in Weston Subedge were not enclosed until 1850, and that parish lies side by side with Saintbury over the slope into the great vale.

BY THE HEATH BARN

As the old trackway of Buckle Street took me away to the open downs, I will return that way from Snowshill to the places I meant chiefly to speak about. Barely a mile from the village, the east road out of Snowshill joins Buckle Street passing northward on its way by Broadway Tower and the Heath Barn to Willersey Hill and Saintbury. It is all a beaten road at this part, but as it is only a lane and is still repaired with the local stone from quarry or field, it keeps its beautiful native colour, a rich orange when wet, and sandy white when powdered by the midsummer sun and traffic into dust as fine as flour. This quiet bit between the trees skirts the brow of the hill, with the slope of Middle Hill on one side and the broken uplands to Seven Wells and Spring Hill to the east on the other. Wood pigeons croon to you, and squirrels scuttle up the trunks and peer at you, until you pretend to threaten them with your stick, when they will run and leap delightfully. Their trapeze feats are amazing where the trees happen to be apart, and the twig they leap for seems so ludicrously insufficient until they hang swinging on it successfully and run along to firmer foothold. I wonder whether one ever misses its grip and falls to the ground? I have watched a good many, but never saw this happen.

It was just across here by Seven Wells that the old main London to Worcester road used to run before the present descent by Broadway Hill was made, and the Fish Inn built, at the end of the eighteenth century.

It formerly dropped down the hill by Coneygree Lane to Broadway Old Church. This is on the westward side of the old Buckle Street, in front of which is spread the great Evesham vale, but on the east you look away over the uplands towards Bourton-on-the-Hill, Moreton-in the-Marsh and the hills which bound the valley of the Evenlode. But close at hand is the lonely little farm known as the Heath Barn, separated from the road by a strip of old beech wood which encircles the rough pasture and the fine patch of furzy heath and elder stretching away towards the fields and grounds of Spring Hill. These latter used to be dotted with beech clumps, which they told me forty years ago had been originally planted in the manner of the various regiments of troops on the field of Waterloo. Possibly it was true, but I never took the trouble to verify the statement.

The very name of the Heath Barn, as well as that beech wood with the tumbled-down mossy wall about it and the fine waste tract in front, always allured me, and no spot could be better for watching several interesting birds and wild things. I once imagined I had saved a thrush there from the fangs of a stoat, but the little hunter might just as well have had his quarry, for the bird, though living with throbbing heart when I handled it, turned its eyes piteously on me and expired almost immediately. I never tried to thwart a stoat again. But yes, once more, and this time a rabbit, but not up here. It was in crossing the Willersey fields to Honeybourne. A sharp scream close by thrilled me, and instinctively I leapt forward with my stick. The stoat fled, and the rabbit, a young one, was floundering in the grass. I foolishly put it in my pocket and carried it home to a box and straw in order to nurse it back to health. But it refused all food, languished, and the next morning was dead. So never again have I tried to play providence to wild victims. With the rabbit, no doubt, I only protracted its agony, for most likely I aroused a more inexplicable terror, and for a longer time, in its stricken heart than the well-known enemy had done. Yet there is something quite intolerable in seeing a stoat stalking a bewildered rabbit right across the open fields. I could never learn how this extraordinary and grossly unfair chase begins. The tragical scream at the end is only too frequent, and although not quite so bad as that of a hare, is bad enough.

The only other thing I will mention here before passing on is the fact that just at the edge of that patch of waste land by the Heath Barn, near the beech wood, there used to be, thirty years ago, the largest bushes, trees I must call them, of the common wild broom that I ever saw, They must have been a great age, but how they came there I don't know, for this is not a broom or foxglove country, though the gorse is abundant enough. I can only suppose that these isolated shrubs were the last relic of some former soil, like the stunted bits of heather (calluna) which you still find lurking in the grass upon Cleeve Cloud. All our standard fioras give the limits of the broom shrub as 3-6ft, and that no doubt is our usual experience. But those I saw up here had got to 10-12ft at least, roughly measured from my own height. They had formed trunks as thick as an ordinary man's arm, the bark bearing a pretty pattern of a kind of spiral diamond-shaped markings, and these trunks, slanting a little, stood out as prominently as the elder tree trunks, for all the lower shrubby nature of the broom had disappeared, the green twigs, besom-like, from branches about halfway up forming only a head to the trunks like any other small tree.

About half a mile from this point you cross over the Oxford and London highway, and come in full view again of old Chipping Campden in its hollow, with the hills of Ebrington and Ilmington beyond. These form the extreme north end of the Cotswolds, dropping down to the valley of the Stour and Stratford-on-Avon on their north-east side. After crossing the highway, I suppose, the present road leaves the track of Buckle Street, which in all probability crossed that first enclosed field on the right to the acute-angled wall terminating the parish of Saintbury, and so continued on the line of the eastern boundary of that parish, marked by the wall until it becomes again the rugged pathway down the hill beside Newcomb, of which I spoke at first, There does not seem to be any enclosure act for Saintbury on record, but these upper roads were all open and unwalled at any rate till the middle of last century. No doubt the old clerk had helped to build those walls, but I never questioned him as to the age of them. The stone at any rate was close at hand, for after passing the lonely farm of Willersey Hill you soon reach the parish quarries of both Willersey and Saintbury, parted only by the road. Many of my talks with the old clerk, in addition to that first one, took place about here, and many a heap of stones by the roadside did I help him to break whilst the conversations went on. He had a small regular wage as roadman, but for breaking the stone he was paid by the cubic yard, it having been measured and stacked in the quarry and from there hauled out to the roadside. He never rose to a higher figure than 10p per cubic yard for breaking. There in the summer days I should find him, seated on a block of stone with a sack for a cushion, and on hearing a footstep the genial old features would be raised with a smile, and together with a polite salute would come in deep clerkly tones, 'Well, well, sir, you have found me again.' This was the usual greeting. He was always alert for a talk with any casual passer-by, but there were very few on that upland road in those days before cars, and many a day would pass without his seeing a single one. If the day was windy or liable to be stormy, you would find him at some more or less sheltered heap nearer home down by the trees, where he was, as he said, 'in the burrow.' I generally heard of any interesting interview he had had with some particular tramp or other visitor. One countryman who occasionally passed him was called by the clerk 'an uncomfortable man,' and as an illustration of this man's taste for discomfort it was stated that 'if he talked to you in the quarry he would choose a three-cornered stone to sit on.' But perhaps this poor old fellow only felt at home in discomfort, for I think it was the same man who, on finding fault with the freedom of his granddaughters gadding about at night, was assailed by the women with a defensive 'You had your day.' 'Iss,' was the retort, 'and a fine day an' all – 'taters and salt.'

Into the old clerk's own speech there entered many a delightful Shakespearean turn of phrase, like that of 'I'll be with you straight,' on my very first visit with him to the church bells. It is needless to say that this was merely his own native language. He never quoted, for he told me he had never read Shakespeare. A very picturesque phrase came from him once when telling me of a visitor he had had who belonged to one of the village families but had left when a youth and had not been back for a good many years. The man did not immediately make himself known, nor did the clerk at once recognise him, though, as he said, 'I knew his type of favour,' meaning, of course, that he was haunted by some family resemblance in his visitor's features. But all the old man's speech was delightful. Never a trace of affectation, as I have already said; his vernacular being merely purged of the grossnesses of local dialect without impairing the charm of its quaint simplicity, so as to suggest constantly what we call Biblical or Shakespearean English. Two or three malapropisms he had, one only of which I will mention here. This was meant for fatality, but was always pronounced as faciality, and was only used in the sense of fate or destiny, and never in my hearing with the journalistic meaning of a fatal occurrence. For instance, if speaking of some infirmity of character, such as habitual drunkenness in a man, he would say 'he seemed to have a faciality on him.' It was interesting to note that the clerk never used the word in the journalistic sense, for I think he must have got it originally from the newspapers and misread it, as he would never have adopted such an original pronunciation if he had heard it used in speech. But anything of the kind was very rare with him, and when it occurred it never arose from total obliviousness of all meaning in the word mispronounced. This latter unconsciously grotesque 'derangement of epitaphs' in the uneducated is not easy to explain when done in all innocence and without any trace of vanity. I suppose in reality it arises from a sense of politeness, a kind of putting on one's Sunday clothes when speaking to a more or less educated person. I think the strongest instance of this I ever met with here came from an old woman several years over eighty, a contemporary of the old clerk, who lived at Saintbury. One day I met her coming down the fields to the village shop in Willersey, and at the parish boundary ditch between Stanthill and Gibbs's Meadow, where was a wicket gate in the hedge, we stood to look at each other. That ditch between us was then always in a bad state, and in wet weather spread to a watery slough just at the pathway. Two or three quite insufficient stepping stones afforded the only insecure footing. As we looked at each other across the mud, the little piping voice came, 'It be almost increditable to pass.' Every syllable was quite clearly enunciated. Why this old lady should have wanted such an elaborate word I can not guess, for I had never before noticed in her any tendency that way.

Only yesterday I got another singular instance in a man whom I should never have suspected of such extraordinary confusion of thought. In this case, although the words wrongly used were real ones, they betrayed a total ignorance of what even the proper words intended were meant to convey. This man, who is only in early middle age and is above the level of much of our rustic intelligence, was telling me about a bird which had been brought in by a cat alive and was rescued by the woman of the house. She tried 'artificial reputation,' the man told me, and the bird revived and was liberated. As may be imagined, it was not respiration at all that was tried. The speaker did not even know the meaning of the word he was attempting to use, but for some reason preferred this way of describing mere tender feeding and petting of the terrified bird. Speaking of a cat reminds me of yet another misapplication of words worth mentioning, used by a woman in whose cottage I was lodging many years ago. But, although as simple a countrywoman, this was altogether on a higher plane, though quite as innocently committed. I had suggested that some food remnants would do for the cat, when my hostess broke into a protestation of what dainties the animal had already secured that day, some of which had been stolen, and ended up with unexpected aptitude, 'So hasn't she fared presumptuously?' Here, the good woman not only showed some knowledge of her Bible, but in attempting to quote it made an even better application than she intended.

But I was looking forward to Willersey quarry when I was drawn into this digression, so I had better let the quarries now open a fresh chapter for themselves. I often used to talk to the clerk about his beautiful stone and the wealth of interesting fossils in it, but neither aspect made much headway with him. Such little geological gossip as I could afford him certainly gave interest for the moment, but it never went so far as to prevent his smashing up next time, quite obliviously, some particularly good specimen. Yet even the smallest power of observation in these rural workers would so brighten their outlook and relieve the deadening effects of toil. Not that they are engrossed in their mere labour, or oppressed by the weight of strenuous muscular exertion. Far from that. That is the result of amateur application to any such job. No daily labour could go on upon such terms, a fact not fully appreciated by some master farmers in allotting a day's work. Nothing is more common than this overestimate of possibilities in one who has lived by directing work without ever having really gone through the mill of doing such work with his own hands, This leads to many unreasonable complaints against good and conscientious men and women. Still, there is a medium. The clerk used to tell me a story (possibly a Joe Miller unknown to me) of a passing parson ending up a talk with a God-bless-your-work to a farm labourer, whose prompt reply was, 'Dunt care, sir, whether ur do or no, I be working by the day.' I have no doubt the good old clerk himself would very much rather have broken the stones by the day than by the cubic yard. There is always that phrase, 'It'll do for now', ready at hand. It was just on the road here, the clerk told me, that once he brought with old Master Somebody a load of stones to repair a broken wall, and as they shot it down the farmer said, 'There, clerk, it'll do for now.' Nearly twenty years afterwards, the old clerk himself broke up that heap of stones for the road, the wall never having been repaired in the meantime.

SEVEN

THE QUARRS

All the villages hereabouts have their parish quarry, or quarr, as it is locally called. This form of the word, oddly enough, is not used by Shakespeare, though it is by Drayton, a Warwickshire man. It is widespread through the west and south-west. Up in Yorkshire, I remember, it is always 'quarrel 'oile' for 'quarry hole'. These Gloucestershire quarries vary much, of course, in size and picturesqueness according to the locality, and there is a good deal of difference, too, in the quality of the stone for different purposes. Certain places like Chipping Campden and Bourton-on-the-Hill gain a peculiar reputation for the quality of their building stone, whilst the beautiful roofing stones, known as Stonesfield slates or slats, are only to be obtained from particular strata. The principal of these in this neighbourhood are at Guiting, and at Eyford, near Stow-on the-Wold, so out of my immediate district.

Mr Guy Dawber gives a good account of the interesting way in which these slates are obtained in his beautifully illustrated volume on the Cotswold Cottages and Farmhouses, which I will take the liberty of quoting. 'In October,' he says, 'a piece of ground at the quarry is measured off, and the upper 8-10ft of loose "brash" is cleared away, this process being called "ridding." The "pendal," as the stone for the slates is called, is then uncovered and wheeled to the top of the ground, laid down flat, and roughly fitted together as nearly as it will allow, in thicknesses varying from 2 to 12 or 14in, just as it comes from the quarry. It has then to lie and wait for the winter frosts, which swell the beds of natural moisture in the "pendal," and when a thaw sets in, a few blows of the hammer soon separate the layers, which are then cut to the sizes required and sorted ready for use, But should the winter be mild, the stone has to wait till the following year.'

And I must apologise for taking the further liberty of adding what Mr Dawber so truly says of these stone roofs themselves. 'For stone houses there is no more beautiful or suitable material than these slates as a roof covering, which harmonize so admirably, and seem almost to grow from the walls supporting them. When old and covered with lichens their colour is indescribably exquisite, and seen in their proper setting amidst trees and fields the general tone of silver grey harmonizes admirably with the surrounding landscape. Even when new they are pleasing, as the slates are of all shades of greys, browns, and yellows.'

It is certainly impossible to exaggerate the beauty of these buildings almost from every point of view, but my purpose just now is to speak of the quarries themselves from which the materials for them are, or have been, obtained. Not only have they supplied the materials for all these beautiful structures, but in doing so have also become very picturesque objects themselves. From the little grass-grown pits in the rough pastures where the dog violet, rock cistus and wild thyme nestle, and out of which no doubt the prehistoric inhabitants made their huts and graves, down to the orange and grey cliffs on which the quarrymen still labour, we find almost every possible grade of size and feature. On the hilltops the stone is so near the surface that you may throw off the few inches of earth anywhere, clear out the chalky brash and few feet of disintegrating stone, and come upon the solid rock immediately. So that in some few cases where no great quarry is contemplated, the stone is just worked perpendicularly downwards and hauled up as from a great shaft. But the most picturesque quarries have gradually eaten their way inwards, so to speak, on the side of some slope opening up all before them, so that a cartway of easy gradient has grown from the mouth, going forward as the excavation widens and deepens, until in a few centuries you arrive at a fine rugged amphitheatre with a cliff of 50ft or more at its deepest part in front of you. Willersey Parish quarry is a beautiful example of this type, up on the hilltop about 900ft above sea level. The old rubble which forms the gradually increasing slope on each side, and the widening margins skirting the cartway, have in course of time got clothed with such grass and flowers as love this stony soil, That wide level floor in front of the semicircular precipice from which the great blocks are dislodged, and which we may well call the arena, for this oolitic stone grinds and weathers down to a layer of beautiful golden sand, is where the stone is stacked and measured ready for removal. It is symmetrically built, a yard high over the whole surface, rectangular, and walled evenly and neatly at the four sides, which of course are regulated in length according to the number of yards required. In this quarry no blasting is necessary, the stone parting naturally into manageable blocks, which are loosened with huge crowbars and broken up below into sizes suitable for stacking.

These are the places where you see how thin is the layer of soil on these Cotswold uplands. Just a few inches only of the loveliest brown earth cover the stone brash with which every ploughed field is spread, and which, as I have said, alone separates it from the rock. Yet this stony soil not only gets covered with a velvet turf, but yields in tillage fine crops of barley, oats, turnips and swedes. It has long been as renowned for its barley as it was for the sheep which first brought wealth to this favoured district. You see acres, too, of that beautiful crimson sainfoin brilliant in the sun, no less than 15 per cent of the whole Cotswold area being devoted, it is said, to this crop. The upper rim of a quarry is, of course, usually protected by wall or fence, and when it is this latter you can often sit down below in the summer sun and see the ripening corn and the red poppies waving up to the very edge against a background of blue sky and white cloud. Always approach a silent quarry carefully, that you may get a good peep of the shy wild things you are almost sure to startle there. Rabbits will scuttle into their burrows; a hare or fox may bound up the slope into the corn; a kestrel or sparrow-hawk will start from the upper rocks, or better still from its meal by some big sitting stone down in the arena. And in the profound silence you will hear the soil and stones rolling down to the bottom which the animals have dislodged. Or, if you want to know how weathering goes on, come on a sunny morning when the sharp frost is giving way, and you will hear incessant movement, often some great block rolling down which the thawing ice has let go and raising a stream of stones and earth in its track.

The road alone parts the Willersey from the Saintbury quarry, the two entrances being nearly opposite. But they are of a totally different type. The Saintbury one is of much more modest proportions, as befits the retiring little parish. The difference, however, is not merely a matter of size. Though only a few yards apart, much of the growth of each is distinct. For some reason trees have fought shy of the promising expanse of the Willersey side; a thorn or two, a palm willow, perhaps half a dozen ash saplings, and not more than two or three still younger beech, being, I believe, the only ones that have gained a foothold there. Saintbury quarry, on the other hand, is getting choked with trees, mostly beech and ash wholly self-sown. The old, long-disused half was years ago planted with larch, but the other part, left to itself and also now disused, has been sown liberally by the south-west wind with beech nuts and ash keys from the parish boundary row. Some of these I saw as saplings years ago, some in their first two leaves, and some as seeds before they had sprouted. If left alone the place will soon be a delightful little beech grove, with that wonderful red carpet of dead leaves in winter which throws out so well the clean, smooth, smoky grey of the beech bark in the sun.

Now, why so very few seeds have germinated twenty yards away on the other, western side of the road I cannot pretend to determine. I have never heard of any human interference. We are taught, it is true, that south-west winds predominate, and the bend of the boundary beech tree heads confirms the fact here, but surely a certain proportion of beech nuts must have been flung those few yards at some time or other in the course of years from the east, to say nothing of the light flaky ash key which is blown for great distances in every direction. The beech, too, is so natural to this soil that it can hardly escape germination anywhere. In some part of almost every bank or field you will find in the spring those uncrumpling, fleshy, embryonic leaves bursting the hard triangular case in which they have been packed with such amazing economy, almost rivalling in wondrous beauty the crumpled poppy bud as it throws the two halves of its cap off in the morning sun, Nonetheless, the beech seems determined to avoid Willersey quarry, or it would have covered the slopes long ago. Nearly all the other things you would expect to find are there. Nowhere does that little tufted gem of the summer days, the bird's-foot trefoil, flourish better – in perfection when hanging over a bit of this golden stone. Less abundant, and less noticeable too, though not less (if differently) beautiful, is its relative the horseshoe vetch, whose head of curly horse-shoe pods for some reason invariably suggested to me in youth that much-caricatured curly head of him we irreverently called Dizzy. The thistles I have already said, are a beautiful feature of these chalky uplands, but it always annoyed me never to find a single plant of the big woolly-headed one in this quarry, although it flourished well a field or two away on Willersey Hill. But the handsome musk or nodding thistle, the rosette of the dwarf or stalkless one, and that shining golden star of the canine never grew better. The beauty of the nodding thistle at every stage of growth is really remarkable. The rosette of leaves it forms the first year, preparatory to blossoming the next, is of matchless delicacy and infinite detail as it unfolds its tender green. A tinge of white down about it, and the intricate spiral arrangement of its host of infant prickles packed so close in the centre, makes the green shine with a silvery bloom. Then, when it rises up and branches into blossom, there are very few more beautiful things in our wild flora, whether in detail or general effect. The gentle bend of the blossom head gives it a positive personal charm like that of the daffodil, but it would be useless to try to convey in words the wonder of the bud or the rich crimson flower, in its halo of numberless sharp-pointed rays of palest green, also spirally or 'quincuncially' arranged. But in looking at this subtle and beautiful arrangement one cannot escape old Sir Thomas Browne again and his 'Quincunx of the Ancients, artificially, naturally, and mystically considered.' It is a tempting subject in itself, and strikes you in nature on every hand. Amidst his numberless natural examples of it, Sir Thomas of course includes these of our thistles, 'the squamous heads of scabious and knapweed,' and 'the thicket on the head of the Teazel.' In the quarry here it has a particularly striking effect in winter on the closed dead heads of the big knapweed, standing up on their dried stalks, the scales of which form a little vase or flask so conspicuously 'lozenge-figured' in black and white. 'In such a grove do walk the little creepers about the head of the burr,' says Sir Thomas, 'and such an order is observed in the aculeous prickly plantation upon the heads of several common thistles, remarkably in the notable palisadoes about the flower of the milk-thistle; and he that inquireth into the little bottom of the globe-thistle may find that gallant bush arise from a scalp of like disposure.'

Since I have wandered again into Sir Thomas I cannot close him without taking a few of his words on the quincunx 'mystically considered' which, of course, carries him far. Having got on the subject of germens and seeds that 'do lie in perpetual shades,' he reflects that 'darkness and light hold interchangeable dominions and alternately rule the seminal state of things.' And this brings him to that fine passage which forestalls the sonnet of Blanco White. 'Light that makes things seen,' says he, 'makes some things invisible. Were it not for Darkness and the shadow of the Earth, the noblest part of the Creation had remained unseen, and the Starrs in Heaven as invisible as on the fourth day, when they were created above the Horizon, with the Sun, or there was not an Eye to behold them. The greatest mystery of Religion is expressed by adumbration, and in the noblest part of Jewish Types we find the Cherubims shadowing the Mercy-seat; Life itself is but the shadow of Death, and Souls departed but the shadows of the Living: All things fall under this Name. The Sun itself is but the dark simulachrum, and Light but the shadow of God.'

And lastly those closing words of his dissertation, which he was evidently writing at midnight, in his house at Norwich there, looking out to the starry sky. 'But the Quincunx of Heaven runs low and 'tis time to close the five ports of knowledge. We are unwilling to spin out our awaking thoughts into the phantasms of sleep, which often continueth praecogitations, making Cables of Cobwebs and Wildernesses of handsome Groves ... Though Somnus in Homer be sent to rouse up Agamemnon, I find no such effects in these drowsie approaches of sleep. To keep our eyes open longer were but to act our Antipodes. The Huntsmen are up in America, and they are already past their first sleep in Persia. But who can be drowsie at that hour which freed us from everlasting sleep or have slumbring thoughts at that time when sleep itself must end, and as some conjecture all shall awake again?'

Nor are the old physician's deep organ tones at all too solemn for the silence even of a simple old quarry. It is indeed hard to escape them in view of the stupendous process so visibly going on before you. Take up the hardest bit of rock flung down here and you can see it is made up of what was life some millions of years ago, and is now only to be ground down again into that beautiful brown earth as a source of renewed life for still fresh centuries. I suppose it is on the later 'living garment' that my own affection is particularly set. And there can be no denying that this clean limestone soil is especially rich in that winsome herbage which goes straight to the heart, and so much of which is doubly endeared to us through Shakespearean and other poetical association. To sit in the sun and look into the meadow grass of a field at the beginning of June, say between Cutsdean and Ford, is really startling even to one accustomed to a little more than a nodding acquaintance with our wild flowers.

Here in the quarry you can almost watch the process of this clothing carried on from the very beginning. As the fresh-thrown rubble is left to settle down at the sides, worms and seeds immediately get to work, and year after year you will see some addition to the first rude, hardy colonists that take possession almost before the quarryman's shovel has moved away. Fortunately nettles (or black 'ettles, as they are called here) do not always get much of a foothold in these places. I am not sure that there are any at all in the Willersey quarry. Their presence is generally a sign of some contributory squalor on the part of man, such as that hideous fate which befalls some old quarries of being made the receptacle for cartloads of worse than rubbish – of broken pots and pans, old kettles, meat tins and boots, with other nameless refuse, in the society of which nettles invariably abound, but which in the summer at all events they do their best to hide. Many District Councils even are guilty of this atrocity, just to avoid the simple and only reasonable expedient of burial.

Thistles soon get in, but as I have said, they are mostly of an attractive kind. The common creeping one is not particularly partial to such places, preferring the neglected pastures, where they become a great pest and one which many farmers seem to have given up all efforts to cope with. Of the others I have said enough, except perhaps the carline. There is a good deal of charm about this one, too, in spite of his stiff unbending habit. It is more enduring than any of them, making bright golden stars of its exhausted seed heads which last all the winter through and shine so brilliantly in the sun. Indeed they are more like a little sun than a star, being just the conventional figure of the sun drawn by the old illustrators, a flat, round, golden plate surrounded by numberless pointed rays. Its name, too, is so interesting, being given from nobody less than Charlemagne, according to the legend quoted by Dr Prior from Tabernaemontanus, who says that 'A horrible pestilence broke out in his army, and carried off many thousand men, which greatly troubled the pious emperor. Wherefore he prayed earnestly to God, and in his sleep there appeared to him an angel, who shot an arrow from a cross-bow, telling him to mark the plant upon which it fell, for that with that plant he might cure his army of the pestilence. And so it really happened.' The herb thus indicated was this thistle. It is a pity that our later pharmacopia will not confirm so romantically attested a virtue.

The scabious and big-rayed purple knapweed will soon follow; a very handsome snow-white variety of this latter I used to find in the Saintbury quarry. Round the feet of these will quickly creep those two charming potentillas, the sweet-scented silver-weed and the cinquefoil, lovely members of that loveliest of all families, the rose, Yellow though they are, they differ in their beautiful shade of yellow, and as it is the commonest of all flower colours so is yellow the most variable in its delicacy of shade. Take the little mouse-ear hawk-weed, for instance, which also follows here quickly in the train, before the slow coarse grass has power to overtake them. This is yellow, too, and may be hurriedly passed over as dandelionish, but look at it again, and both in colour and gesture it will be at once seen to have charming distinction. In bud it is simply exquisite, with its crimson-tipped petals gathered up like a little round mouth, and when expanded, so that the crimson is not seen, the solitary flower on its bare unbranched little stalk of a few inches high, rising from its silky-haired leaves, is of the most delicate lemon yellow, as far removed as can be from its coarser relatives of the railway embankments.

But I must get on. Of all the interesting practical work of the quarries I have said nothing, nor of the subtle association of the material they supply with the development of the beautiful domestic architecture of the neighbourhood. The stone itself apparently inspired the rustic craftsmen with their genius for its consummate handling. This genius grew from the soil, and is as native and peculiar to it as the very flowers that beautify its surface, and all these things combine to produce a simple and homely charm to which the eyes of a feverish world may look sadly and wistfully back.

EIGHT

DREAM-STUFF

A little way below the quarries, four roads meet at the top of Wilersey Bank. Here are Gunn's cottages, where the old clerk lived in boyhood, and the road going east which passes them skirts the wall of Newcomb and Weston Park on its way to Chipping Campden and Mickleton. As leading also to Dover's Hill one would imagine there must always have been a track here, although the old 1in ordnance map does not even give dotted lines for one between Newcomb and the top of Dyer's Lane coming up from Campden. I wish I had asked the old clerk all about it, for there is little doubt that he must have helped to construct the present road. It was evidently made about 1850, when the Weston Enclosure Act was passed, as was also the descent into Weston Subedge village from Dover's Hill, since the old ordnance map gives no dotted track for this one either.

In any case this road from Gunn's along the ridge is interesting, as it connects us with the musical old name of Kiftsgate, which the hundred still bears, as well as leads to the wonderful old town of Chipping Campden. After passing Newcomb gateway and wall it crosses at right angles the old trackway of Buckle Street, where this emerges from the trees on the brow of the hill, marking the boundary between the parishes of Saintbury and Weston Subedge. At this point the road is nobly over-arched by two fine beech trees on the parish boundary line, whose branches mingle overhead so as to form an impressive entrance to Weston parish. Happily these two trees were spared, but the best of these boundary beeches, as well as the fine grove of them at the back of Newcomb House, were felled several years ago. I believe the old clerk told me that they had been planted by the member of the Roberts family who was squire at Comb in the first years of the nineteenth century. Just beyond, by the roadside, is the little Weston quarry from which no doubt the stone was obtained for building this road originally as well as the walls enclosing it, and as it remains a by-road at this part it is repaired from here still and so keeps the beautiful orange colour which has been lost on the main roads owing to the use of Shropshire granite or tar.

This bit towards Dover's Hill is called the Long Hill, and formerly went by the name of the Narrows. It is near here that the old Kiftsgate Stone still stands, the ancient meeting place of the hundred, and with this locality the name itself seems to be associated, for one etymological explanation claims Kiftsgate (anciently Cheftesihat) to mean Narrow Way, 'because this hundred is connected with the main body of the county by a neck of land barely a hundred yards across.' This might well apply to the original extent of the hundred, for it has been considerably enlarged since the *Domesday Book* by the absorption of other hundreds of independent existence then. It now stretches some miles even beyond Winchcomb. In Taylor's *Domesday Survey of Gloucestershire*, it is explained thus: 'Cheftesihat Hundred, with its member Mene, seems to have consisted of a part of Longborough, and to this in the Conqueror's time the sheriff had added the lordship of two hundreds, no doubt Celflede and Wideles. To Winchcomb, at the time of Domesday, had been added three hundreds, the hundred of the town itself, Holeford and Gretestanes; and this group being in later times added to the Cheftesihat Hundreds, the one great hundred of Kiftsgate was formed, containing one tenth of the whole county. The meeting-place for the hundred of Kiftsgate was at a gate above Weston Subedge. This would have been near the boundary between Celflede and Wideles hundreds, and it may have been the meeting-place of one of them before they were united, at any rate it would be as convenient a place as any other for the men of both those hundreds, and also for those of all the hundreds which afterwards took their name from Kiftsgate.'

It is perilous to meddle with etymology nowadays, but I suppose it is probable that the first half of this name is connected with the Celtic word 'cefn', a ridge, still in common use in Wales, and lingering also in our Cheviots as well as in 'Chevin', a hill name at Otley in Yorkshire and in Derbyshire. As to the second half, it is, perhaps, hardly necessary to say that it has nothing to do with a gate in our present sense of the word.

In old names the word always signifies a passage, road or street. So I suppose our Kiftsgate would simply mean 'Ridgeway', a name certainly applicable enough to the site of this central meeting place of the hundred. If it is not disrespectful to say so, there is therefore something comical in a late president of the county archaeologists several years ago lamenting in his address, with reference to this old Kiftsgate stone, that 'the gate, alas, has gone, the post alone remains.' But he adds to this an interesting association of later days when he says: 'I have reason to believe that formerly the kings of England on their coronation were proclaimed kings on this very spot, for it fell to my lot to have to take the evidence of an old man named Gould, who died in the year 1850, aged 98, who remembered this ceremony when George III came to the throne.' And with the expiration of this lingering ceremony I suppose at last died out all remembrance of this important local meeting place, which must have witnessed such picturesque and dramatic scenes since the institution of that 'hundred' by those West Saxon Hwiccas, who had come marauding up from the south-west.

Although we have here got fairly to the brow of the hills, all view of the great vale is hidden by the trees which skirt the road on your left nearly all the way to Dover's Hill. On the other side, however, the slope is more open and a peep can be got of the grey old wool town of Chipping Campden, slumbering so peacefully in its hollow. This is such a dreamlike spot that, since I cannot say here a great deal about it, possibly I should pass it by altogether. But this I positively cannot do. Once more I must in fancy stand at that truly Gloucestershire stile and drop down through the fields into the long silent street which has never lost for me that spell of enchantment under which it seemed to lie when I first entered it as a boy. No imagination was needed. Here was the old world itself, touched by a magic wand centuries ago and still remaining spellbound. After hours of sunlight on these lonely hills with the skylarks and the plovers, late in the afternoon I saw below me this wide secluded basin, made as it seemed simply to catch the sun, and basking there in the radiance was the little grey town with a majestic church tower shining at one end of it. Gradually I descended into the hollow, and on entering that one wide street, swept by the sun from behind me, I tried to muffle my footsteps in the silence. At the market place I stood in silent astonishment. From end to end nobody was to be seen. My foot alone on the gilded pavement (all consisting then not of cement but of the dove-grey lias stone) had broken the quiet of immemorial sleep and my own sounds only had echoed around me. Between the church tower and the sun lay the antique town in one graceful curve of what seemed infinite detail and variety yet of matchless

1 The village of Uley.

2 The Windrush Way.

Above: 3 The Cotswold countryside. (© Emily Locke)

Left: 4 Arlingham. (© Emily Locke)

Above: 5 Pittville Pump
Room, Cheltenham.
(© Alan Pilbeam)

Right: 6 Saintbury Church.
(© Graham Martin)

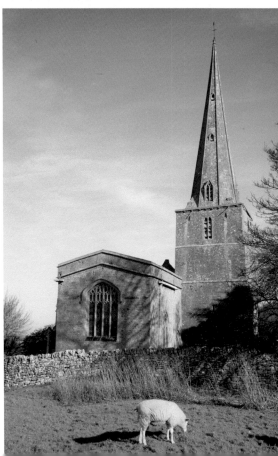

7 Winchcombe.

8 Winchcombe.

9 Broadway Tower. (© Alan Pilbeam)

10 Birdlip Hill. (© Regina Knut)

11 The Malvern Hills. (© Stuart Herbert)

Above: 12 Berkeley Castle.
(© Nick Kaye)

Right: 13 Berkeley Castle.
(© Chris Price)

harmony. Built all of stone, turned absolutely to gold just then, this wide street widened still more midway to admit, as islands, the arched, pillared and gabled Market Hall and the Gothically-buttressed Guildhall. It was indescribable, simply a dream. Even after getting over the first impression of the sleeping princess somewhere whom you were destined to arouse and deliver from the age-long spell, how could you sink much beyond looking at any rate for Shakespeare, Ben Jonson, or at least Master Endymion Porter, to accost you from one of those ancient doorways? Anything later was out of the question, impossible. No, one can ask nothing better than to find such a place thus absolutely dreamlike and solitary on a first visit. The effect is startling and happily you never lose it. It is behind all future visits. Whether the place is under a spell or no, at least you are. Without distractions you can afterwards trace at leisure all the little rills of life that have trickled down for centuries through the moss-grown channels, and which there stand crystallised as it were into imperishable pictures.

A place like Chipping Campden affords an epitome of so many of these centuries of national life, nearly all the sources of which are represented there. Not only do the old stones record them, but old crafts still linger, old words, old habits, old beliefs, are firmly implanted. The name of the place itself goes back almost to the time of Kiftsgate. This was at first Campden merely, otherwise Kampedene, 'the battle valley,' a brief but significant record of some notable bloodshed on the site, claimed to be dimly recorded in history, and still lingering here not only in the name of the town but in that of Battle Bridge also, a spot beside a brook in the green hollow traversed by the present road past the railway station towards Ebrington. 'It is remarkable,' says the late Professor Skeat, "that *camp* in middle-English never has the modern sense, but is only used in the sense of fight or battle.' So Campsted meant a battle ground, as Campden a battle valley. Much later came the epithet Chipping to modify the original word. This is pretty well known to be equivalent to 'market' merely, a title of new commercial dignity assumed after the town's first charter of the twelfth century. The meaning of this old word is very picturesquely illustrated in Wicliffe's Bible where he translates Luke vii. 32, 'They ben like children sitting in chepinge and speaking togidre.'

This original charter of Campden was confirmed and extended by Henry III on 16 April 1247. By this the place was granted a market on Wednesdays and a fair for three days, at St James's day and two following days, the burgesses also being freed from tolls in markets and fairs. When Edward I appointed commissioners to inquire into local abuses, however, they find that the town of 'Caumpdene hath assize of bread and beer, by what warrant they are ignorant and how long … They say that when the marshals of the lord king came to the market of Caumpdene to view the measures, to correct the false and retain the good, after the departure of the said marshals they again resume the false and put away the good contrary to the provision of the marshals.' So it is, perhaps, consoling to know that in spite of their picturesqueness our forefathers were no better than ourselves. Whether they became more honest or no they at all events gathered riches. Flocks multiplied on the wolds; quarries were unearthed to build not a statelier church only, but Guildhall and several select residences. The two mills recorded in the *Domesday Book* had become four by the end of the twelfth century. Discerning burgesses soon saw the direction in which their prosperity lay, and by the fourteenth century, our old poet Chaucer's time, this battle valley had become one of the busiest centres of the wool trade in all England. An interesting glimpse of the citizens' impatience at being disturbed in their business affairs is got in the fact that the sheriff of Gloucester had to amerce the borough of Campden in 20s and cause Walter the miller of the same town to be distrained of one horse of the value of half a mark, in consequence of the burgesses refusing to answer summons more than twice, instead of four times, a year at the hundred of Kiftsgate.

Another sign of prosperity, too, appears in their obtaining a further grant on 26 May 1360 for an additional fair of three days annually on the eve, day and morrow of St George. It is possible that the energetic young wool stapler William Grevel had some hand in procuring this, for he was buying property in Campden as early as 1367. It was in this man, and during the latter years of this century, that the wool trade here reached its height. Campden became not only the trading centre for the Cotswold wool, but for almost the whole of the wool produced in Wales also. The actual residence of this William Grevel still stands by the pavement of the High Street, a beautiful three-gabled structure of those prosperous wool days of 1390 or thereabouts. To our limited ideas it may have an ecclesiastical appearance, with its perpendicular doorway and panelled bay windows of two storeys, carved and gargoyled. But architectural beauty was a thing also to be had at home in those days. He gave liberally to the building of the church as well, where by will he desired to be buried, and most of the present building is of his time. He was exactly contemporary with Chaucer, dying one year after the poet, in 1401, so he is a figure that can be very vividly recalled. Indeed on the chancel floor of the church lies his effigy in brass to help us, nearly life size, with his wife Marion beside him, under beautiful canopies of inlaid brass also, and in the surrounding inscription in Latin he is honourably recorded as 'a citizen of London and flower of the wool merchants of the whole of England.' From this grave he still calmly looks at you. With close-cropped hair and the 'forked berd' of Chaucer's merchant, he has naturally in that position doffed his 'Flaunderish beaver hat.' Over an undergarment, which can be seen buttoned at the wrists, he wears his tunic reaching to the feet and gathered in at the waist by an ornate girdle from which his dagger hangs, proof that all were not so peacefully minded as himself between Campden and Cheapside. He wears his cloak, too, buttoned over his right shoulder and gracefully hanging over his left arm. On his feet you see 'his botes clasped faire and fetisly,' and 'his resons' no doubt he would still if it were possible speak 'ful solempnely.'

200 years were to elapse, just until our other poet Shakespeare's time, before a still more magnificent merchant was to put the finishing touches to Chipping Campden as we now see it. But he came under very different circumstances from William Grevel, being already an opulent patron and magnate, and not personally associated with the commercial prosperity of the town. This Sir Baptist Hicks, the London mercer and money-lender of kings and princes, is better known than the wool stapler, and can also be seen in another part of the church in all the dignity of statuesque marble and pillared canopy. His pomp is somewhat oppressive and he invites no familiarity. Still no wanderer to Chipping Campden will be the less grateful to him for that, or will fail to lament the catastrophe which was to befall, so soon after his death, the palace he erected for the foundation of his family. In looking at the few ruined stones of this which alone remain, side by side with the beautiful almshouses he founded and endowed, as well as the Market Hall he erected, which still adds so greatly to the charm of his old town, it is hardly possible to escape a thought of the old moralising epitaph on having, saving and losing, which has here been so literally fulfilled. It is only that which he thought most permanent, and in which no doubt he took most pride, that has entirely vanished. Within twenty years of its founder's death, the great mansion lay a heap of smouldering ashes.

Around these two prominent shades does this wondrous old town gather, but since I have gone into such things at all, it is not possible to omit one more who came almost exactly between the two. One would like to know more of Master John Fereby and his good wife Margery, who in the year 1487 founded and endowed the Grammar School, still existing though rebuilt. But of these the centuries, and even the church, seem stubbornly silent. Nonetheless their work and honour remain in good Cotswold stone and in boys' lives and voices. But as I have said, age and beauty consecrate almost every dwelling in the town, few of which are later than the seventeenth century. So at least I am pleased to imagine, but no doubt as elsewhere Chipping Campden moves with the times. For me that golden vignette remains, my footfall alone echoes along the smooth blue lias pavement, the princess and all her retainers still sleep under their magic spell, and I am content to slink away up the fields again, and think what I like of it all from that cumbrous upland stile whence I started. Lots of other associations I have with that old stile, dating from many years later, but I must only recall one. Though it does its best to block the way to the footpath down the fields, it is by no means one of the new methods of deterring passengers. It is just a normal stile of this hill country, and consists simply of a natural slab of stone from the quarry, set up on end, some 4ft sq. and 6in thick – indeed, exactly such a stone as the prehistoric inhabitants chose for squaring their graves and closing the entrances to their burial places. In the twilight one evening, after leaving Campden and climbing the fields, with my back to the east on the way to Willersey, I sat on this stone and turned to take another look at the gathering shades in the valley. The last rosy flush which sunset sometimes throws right across to the east had died away, a thrush was still singing, and out of the mystery over the hollow, from behind the dim Ebrington hills, the solemn full Easter moon like a great golden plate had just risen cloudless and stared at me. A breeze rustled in the Weston trees behind, and there was the old town in the valley. So for me the words of Browning's Arab physician for ever cling to that stile:

> I met him thus:
> I crossed a ridge of short sharp broken hills
> Like an old lion's cheek teeth. Out there came
> A moon made like a face with certain spots
> Multiform, manifold, and menacing;
> Then a wind rose behind me. So we met
> In this old sleepy town at unaware,
> The man and I.

NINE

DOVER'S HILL

S o much has been written about the celebrated Cotswold Games on
Dover's Hill that I need not linger over them, since I have nothing
new to add. It is well known that they were instituted by one Robert
Dover, an attorney of Barton-on-the-Heath in Warwickshire, a village
some miles south-east from here beyond Moreton-in-the-Marsh. By no
means a typical attorney, he is characterised in some manuscript verses
attached to a copy of the *Annalia Dubrensia* in the British Museum (quoted
in the *Dictionary of National Biography*) as:

> Dover that his knowledge not Imploy's
> T'increase his Neighbors Quarrels but their Joyes.

To which is further added in a footnote, 'he was bred an attorney who
never try'd but two causes, always made up the difference.' So having
what he considered a sufficient fortune he soon relinquished even this
pretence to practice and retired to Winchcomb. Then he built himself a
house at Stanway where he died many years later, just as the great Civil
War was beginning. But it was about 1604 that he founded the Cotswold
Games that live with his name, it is said as a practical protest against
the sour puritanical habits which were making their way amongst the
people. He lived to preside over this annual function for more than forty

years, a dignified and venerable figure seated on a white horse in all the glory of regal attire, having secured garments from the wardrobe of King James I through the good offices of Mr Endymion Porter, Groom of the Bedchamber. I don't know what personal association between the attorney and Mr Porter is on record, but presumably it was at the instigation or at least under the countenance of the latter gentleman that this particular spot was chosen for the celebrations, since Mr Porter was born and possessed a patrimonial estate at Aston Subedge in the immediate vicinity. Indeed, there can be little doubt that much of the celebrity these games acquired must have come through this connoisseur in literature and art, the friend and patron of poets.

The lane comes up from Campden, scarcely a mile below, to join this road along the ridge, and between there and the abrupt brow of the hill facing north-west lies the expanse known as Dover's Hill. Although Campden is in a hollow it must be remembered it is a hill town and stands 400-500ft above sea level, and Dover's Hill about 800ft. So it was a fine breezy spot for vigorous exercises on the Thursday and Friday in Whitsun week. Here on the skyline was annually erected a wooden castle turning on a pivot, whence guns were fired to announce the opening of the sports. Of these there was choice enough, and competitors were enticed by a goodly array of prizes. Some of these earliest games mentioned are cudgel playing, wrestling, the quintain, leaping, pitching the bar and hammer, handling the pike, playing at balloon or hand ball, leaping over each other (leap frog, I suppose), walking on the hands, a country dance of virgins, men hunting the hare, which by Dover's orders was not to be killed, and horse-racing on a course some miles long. Choice enough, in all conscience, for every taste. The very list brings back the breeze and the gloriously wild and open state of the country then. No doubt the miles of horse-racing would lie across the Kiftsgate ridge to Broadway Hill, the Heath Barn, and Snowshill, and possibly back by Condicote and Stow-on-the-Wold. Nearly all was open sheep down then and for long after. The hours of those two Whitsun days must have been amply full. But then so was the whole country year of those days, grumble how we will at the poverty and hardships of the rustics' lives. Just go through that epitome of the sporting side of 'The Country Life' that old Herrick dangles so temptingly, and so ineffectually, in the eyes of his courtier friend and patron, 'the Honoured Mr Endymion Porter, Groom of the Bedchamber to His Majesty.'

For sports, for pageantry, and plays,
Thou hast thy eves and holidays,
On which the young men and maids meet
To exercise their dancing feet,
Tripping the comely country round
With daffodils and daisies crowned.
Thy wakes, they quintals, here thou hast,
Thy Maypoles too with garlands graced,
Thy morris-dance, thy Whitsun-ale,
Thy shearing feast, which never fail,
Thy harvest home, they wassail bowl,
That's tossed up after fox-i'-th'-hole,
Thy mummeries, thy Twelfthtide kings
And queens, thy Christmas revellings,
Thy nut-brown mirth, thy russet wit,
And no man pays too dear for it.

But the affluent Mr Porter's die in life was cast and he could not escape it. There was to be no rural ease and quiet for him, not even for his last days. As he had shared in the pomp and intrigues of the court, so had he to drink with it the cup of bitterness. At the end, as he recalled those days of Dover's Hill and little Aston Subedge, did he ever think with a sigh of those opening lines of Robert Herrick's enticing address to him?

Sweet country life, to such unknown
Whose lives are others', not their own,
But, serving courts and cities, be
Less happy, less enjoying thee.

As the death of Robert Dover must have marked the decline of these hill games, so no doubt the troubles of the Civil War brought them to an end. Even fire and sword stalked grimly through this very district, achieving amongst other things that tragical destruction of the mansion of Baptist Hicks down in the hollow, as already mentioned. It is true at the Restoration Dover's Hill emerged once more, but with nothing like its former brilliance, and it soon seems to have died out again. At some later time there was yet another revival, for it survived as an annual event until 1851, when the late Canon Bourne, rector of Weston Subedge, no doubt rightly concluded that what it had become must end. The industrial curse had by then come upon us, and in any case there was no Captain Dover with his regal presence and on his white horse to control and regulate the proceedings. The old clerk of Saintbury told me that in his youth neighbourly grudges and quarrels would be nursed for Dover's Hill, and be there worked off in nothing less than trial by combat under the guise of sport. Even he did not in the least lament the cessation of the games and fully admitted the disgraceful scenes to which they gave rise. Canon Bourne has left on record his own estimate and the action he felt compelled to take in the interests of his own parish and of public morality. 'Dover's Hill,' he says, 'became a meeting of the lowest characters merely for debauchery. During Whitsun week the residuum of the black country came there. I have seen as many as thirty thousand, but I am told that many more were assembled. The whole district became demoralised and I determined if possible to stop this evil. An Act was passed for the division and enclosure of the hill and the last Dover's meeting was held in 1851.' So that was the end of it all, as of so much else originally inspired by good intentions. To conclude my own brief survey of the thing, I will reproduce an old bill of the later celebrations formerly in the possession of Canon Bourne.

DOVER'S ANCIENT MEETING

1812

On Thursday in Whit-week

on that

highly renowned and universally admired spot Dover's Hill

near

Chipping Campden, Glos.

The sports will commence

with a good match of Backswords

for a purse of guineas

To be played by 9 or 7 men on a side, Each side

must appear in the ring by 3 o'clock in the afternoon

or 15s., each pair will be given

for as many as will play.

Wrestling

for belts and other prizes

also

Jumping in bags and Dancing And a Jingling Match for 10/6

As well as divers others of celebrated

Cotswold and Olympic games
for which this annual
meeting has been
famed for centuries.

T. CHAMBERLAINE, *Steward*.
R. ANDREWS, *Clerk*.

Although the hill is enclosed and divided, the front part of it is still a fine green pasture, level and open for a quarter of a mile or more at the top and dropping abruptly some hundreds of feet to the villages of Weston and Aston Subedge nestling in the trees below. The face of it forms a great semicircular amphitheatre, all unenclosed green, which I suppose is a natural escarpment, but it looks as if it might have been a vast quarry some centuries ago. A few very fine old thorn trees are sprinkled on the slope, but the lower part becomes a wild hawthorn brake known as the Linches.

At Whitsuntide, when the old revels were held, surely some of the participants must have found a stray thought for this expanse of fair earth and sky, which would at that time of the year be usually presented from that hilltop. It is impressive enough at any time, but in that heyday of late spring, just as the may blossom and cowslips are over, and the full flood of early summer bloom is about to sweep over those meadows and woods, the effect is such as the most insensate could not wholly escape whether conscious of it or not. You get a north-west day or two about that time which surely touch the highest point of the natural beauty possible to this world of ours. Few spots can lend themselves more completely to such a display than this at the very heart of England. For miles and miles in every direction you see pure and spotless landscape, bounded by blue and mystic hills giving just that touch of romance to which the soft luxuriant foreground does not pretend. Under those wonderful clouds which a north-west breeze alone knows how to carve, glistening on a purity of blue which its breath alone can command, you are caught in a torrent of skylarks' song which seems to fall on every sense quite as fully as on the ear. I believe one who knew.

Wordsworth personally considered his ear to have been his strongest sense, and one can readily accept that. For to what else is not the ear the key? And more particularly amidst that sublime silence in which Wordsworth habitually dwelt.

Such then is the old Dover's Hill, placed here just at the extreme north-east end of the Cotswold Hills. From this point the land falls gradually in the course of a few miles to Stratford-on-Avon, and on the east more irregularly to the little valley of the Stour. There can be no doubt that Shakespeare himself traversed more than once that road round Meon Hill and Mickleton on his way to the Cotswold Games, unless he preferred the uplands by Quinton and Hidcote. Either way we know what eye and ear were to him on the journey. Nor on the journey only. In that motley Elizabethan and early Stuart crowd nothing escaped him, and even now, in the sunny silence, through his wand we can still re-people the hill with more than shades, and behold the revels as clearly as, and certainly more comfortably than, if jostled by the actual crowd.

> This done, then to th' enamelled meads
> Thou goest, and as thy foot there treads
> Thou seest a present Godlike power
> Imprinted in each herb and flower,
> And smell'st the breath of great-eyed kine,
> Sweet as the blossoms of the vine.

TEN

THE LOW ROAD

From the east end of this great amphitheatre of Dover's Hill, a track leads you down the slope through these same enamelled meads to the village of Aston Subedge, and the hill country is at once left behind. The great vale stretching away to Evesham and Worcester is before you, and along the foot of the hills runs the lower road connecting that wonderful string of villages, about a mile apart all the way to Winchcomb and Cheltenham. Still they are hill villages insomuch as they are built of stone from the quarries, with very few of the black timber and thatch which characterise the vale, but otherwise life in such lush and sheltered places has, of course, been very different from that up on the open wold. The change is seen and felt immediately. The enormous elm trees of a rich clay soil tower overhead. Orchard trees are luxuriant, and the trunks green with moss and lichen fostered by the mild and humid air. The kine and poultry have a sleek and leisurely demeanour which suggests easy terms with life and nature generally. The human homes appear snug almost to indolence, as if fruit and honey dropped from the branches to the lips without the need of so much as a hand to reach them. The air is full of scent, blending a little too much at times with the vapour of last year's leaf mould perhaps, but this is overpowered in spring by violets and gilliflowers; by roses and honeysuckle, pinks, peonies and madonna lilies in summer; and very often right up to Christmas by stocks and

chrysanthemums and many another cottage flower that has not given in
to an October frost.

In the midst of all this, here at Aston Subedge, Master Endymion
Porter was born. It is a name well known to those who have dabbled
in the literature of the Stuart times. Through an ancestress Porter had
Spanish associations, and very early he was taken off to be brought up in
Spain. This naturally moulded his tastes and disposition, and through a
connection with the royal favourite Buckingham, Endymion was soon
drawn completely into court life. The beautiful old gabled manor house in
which he was born, and which remained his property to the end of his life,
still stands here unaltered, but in person he cannot have been much under
its roof after childhood. I have not seen it mentioned when his father
Edmund Porter died, who had married a cousin, Angela Porter, from the
adjoining parish of Mickleton. But through this parentage Endymion was
essentially a local man, though no poetical allurements could tempt him
to leave his active career for the simplicities of a Cotswold gentleman's
estate. Nonetheless, either he or his lady was by no means averse from
receiving in town gifts of a seasonable rural sort from friends in the
country. We get a delightful glimpse of Sir William Calley, of Burdrop
Park on the Wiltshire Downs, sending up to the Porters by waggoner
for Christmastide 'four collars of brawn, two dozen hogs' pudding, half
white and half black, and a fat young swan,' with other good things,
supplemented a week later by Lady Calley's present of 'a small rundlet of
Metheglin.' In 1628, too, Sir William wrote to Endymion Porter how he
had met Endymion's brother-in-law Canning at Stow Fair on May Day,
and had rode with him to his house at Foxcote, adding that he does not
mean to come to London this term by reason of the foggy air, but hopes
to see Endyniion and his wife in the Long Vacation. Stow Fair, by the by,
is still held on May Day, though now, of course, it is the 12th, Old May
Day, owing to the alteration of the calendar, and it is by this event that we
usually regulate our planting of kidney beans hereabouts. Whilst speaking
of this change of calendar, I may as well mention here that the old clerk
of Saintbury told me he knew an old man, whose name I forget, who
remembered this change being publicly proclaimed from Saintbury Cross
in 1752. Of course, a much greater length of time than this can be spanned
by three minds, but it seemed impressive to me.

As so little is lacking to a singularly charming village, it is unfortunate
that the parish church of Aston is such an insignificant little modern
building without architectural pretensions of any sort. I do not know how
it has come about in a district of such beautiful churches, great and small.

The parish is an ancient one, and the benefice is a rectory, yet not only has any old church there may have been totally disappeared, but also there was apparently never any sort of residence for the incumbent. There used to be, in the Mickleton parish chest, an old register belonging to Aston which goes back as far as 1539, the year after the order issued about them by Thomas Cromwell under Henry VIII, and which was taken away, no doubt, when Aston parish was served by the incumbent of Mickleton. This was the arrangement for many years, and in 1870 the living was in the hands of the headmaster of Campden Grammar School. So, small though it is, Aston appears to have received hardly its fair share of clerical attention through a good deal of its existence. Not having a church tower it has no church bells, and the absence of these is in itself a sad want in the life of such a village. Nearly all of these parishes have beautiful peals of five or six bells, and whether the inhabitants have been conscious of it or not, these have entered very largely into the spirit of their lives. The eloquent power of these bells in giving expression to many simple human emotions needs no remark to those whose ears are attuned to something more than those appalling mechanical appliances common in town belfries. There is only a road between the beautiful old house which was Endymion Porter's and this poor little apology for a church, so the contrast is particularly striking. The quiet dignity of the mullioned and gabled homestead, as of so many other old homes in the village, is happily still unimpaired. I am not aware that there is any record of Porter's actually entertaining any of his literary friends under his roof here when attending the Dover's Hill celebrations, but I suppose it is highly probable. That handful of verses by the principal contemporary poets, printed under the title of *Annalia Dubrensia*, in praise of Dover and his sports, gives proof of personal association with their 'jovial good friend Mr Robert Dover,' as Ben Jonson calls him. But death and calamity broke up the good company, and the Civil War left the affluent courtier not only impoverished but insolvent. This Aston Subedge property of his was sold immediately after his death in 1649. He died in London and was buried at St Martin's-in-the-Fields on 20 August of that year. Like so many other old manor houses, it is now, I believe, a farmhouse.

One of the main thoroughfares to the vale from Chipping Campden and the hill generally comes down Aston Bank, and passing through the village here joins the low road as it trails east and west along the foot of these steep, wooded slopes. Winding with the outline of the hills, and throwing offshoots on either hand to the vale and up into the coombs, this road links village with village in a delightful way. There is something fascinating in the mere subject of a road. It attacks you at so many points. Not only does it call up all the wayfaring life that has for centuries jogged along it, but forces on you alluring visions of those numberless haunts of ancient peace with which our landscape is studded, and which no lifetime could ever be long enough to explore. Then 'longen folk to goon on pilgrimages,' and to keep on going until a few at least of the nooks have yielded up some of the secrets of those centuries which have hallowed their quiet life, and shown a bit of the inexhaustible natural beauties which gladden the very simplest of purely country lanes. It is no good grumbling about the desecration of our quiet roads by the noise and dirt of alien traffic which has at last taken possession of them. We must make the best of it, and slink as far as possible into impracticable byways if we want to study or enjoy the last relics of our wild or picturesque life. In such later development this low road has, of course, suffered in common with the rest. Not only have the unnatural smells and uproar driven so much charming life from the hedgerows, but in most cases the very hedgerows themselves as well as the wayside flowers are gone, through the ruthless widening and tidying, rolling and tarring which such traffic demands. Happily, from Aston to the next village of Weston, there is a direct field path, or used to be, and a still more beautiful and varied one from Weston to Saintbury. But, after all, it is too bad that one should have deliberately to avoid a country road, except for mere purposes of passing from place to place. Indeed, by avoiding this low road the natural approach to Weston Subedge and Saintbury from these lower lands would be missed altogether. The most charming bit of Weston architecturally is at a right angle of this road itself as it passes through the village. But, like Aston, it is all delightful and full of interest. I have already spoken of the hill portion of the parish, embracing Dover's Hill and the fine wood on the slope known as Weston Park which used to fill the whole coomb with magnificent trees. One of the noblest beech trees I ever saw occupied a space to itself in the centre of the wood, the other trees seeming to draw back a little in awe or respect for this ideally developed giant of their race. I remember hearing the axe in Weston Park years ago, but never ventured there to see the battlefield. From a distance, however, the place still presents the appearance of a wood or coppice.

The road which branches off to the church and upper part of the village has, since the Enclosure Act of 1850, been carried on as a highway, passing over the hill to Campden. As in some other of these parishes the church holds itself aloof from the general village, having been built close to the lordly residence which dominated the manor. This latter edifice here has entirely disappeared, but its moat still remains in a field by the church, and it is said for centuries to have been a residence of the Bishops of Worcester. One point of special interest about Weston is the late date of the enclosure of its open and common fields, and the consequent preservation of comparatively recent documents relating to that ancient system. But I must not touch upon that here. The old clerk of Saintbury used to talk to me about Giles Cockbill, the last hayward (hay'ard) of the open fields, evidently a typical old countryman. He and another old man had lived in two adjoining cottages at Weston for fifty years when the property eventually changed hands. The new purchaser had bought them in order to pull the cottages down, and when the two tenants received peremptory notice to quit, the clerk reported Giles as saying to the new owner, 'Well, where be us to gwoa?'

'Go anywhere,' was the prompt retort, which the old clerk not unnaturally considered to be 'a hard speech.'

Giles, for his part, went over the bill to Campden, and was ultimately engaged by a grocer as 'arrands man,' going in such employment round all the adjoining villages delivering goods. I do not remember that Giles was anything of a musician, but the clerk himself possessed the piccolo which had belonged to the last hayward of the next parish, Honeybourne, who had habitually entertained himself by playing upon it as he sat on a bank watching the herds, to keep the cows off the meadow and the sheep off the corn. But I have no doubt that both he and Giles Cockbill would occasionally be found on a hot summer's day, like any Little Boy Blue, 'under a haycock fast asleep.'

Here on the sheltered luxuriant lower lands, we seem in the very atmosphere of these mossy old nursery rhymes. One or other of them is constantly suggested by some pastoral vignette, or some phrase of an inhabitant. Or I am afraid I ought again to say, used to be so, for the changes are very sudden and startling in many ways besides the condition of the roads. So much more self-consciousness has swept over even the most secluded byways, which I suppose we may welcome as progress if we like, but the culture imparted to this awakening by the Sunday newspapers, the cheaper daily press and the cinema, which are our main sources of education after fourteen, will scarcely help to confirm and widen the simple virtues which have confessedly built up our national character. This may no doubt be flouted as the cheap commonplace carping of all fossilised minds. But it surely goes deeper than that. I see the new recipe for resuscitating farm life lies in the phrase 'taking the long view.' This is frankly explained as meaning that all these trees are to be felled, hedges stubbed up and little homesteads obliterated for the purpose of instituting open ranch life on our English soil, so that the latest development in machinery may hum over the 100 acres at a time without any petty hindrances. The small paddock, orchard and cow close, with the blockhead or two who muddle on them, are an anachronism, which makes it impossible to get the full value out of our invaluable land. Such a proposal might really be taken as a comical satire on current tendencies by some medieval reactionary. But it is nothing of the kind. The scheme was not propounded in *Punch*. It is advocated in all seriousness by agricultural authorities and temperately discussed in our first of journals. Is any deep concern therefore for our rural life and culture cheap and commonplace? Can any feeling for all that is most sacred and precious in our national life be expressed too trenchantly or too frequently? If such a 'long view' can be seriously propounded by anybody associated with the practical administration of our agriculture, must not every infant in the village schools be at once aroused to the danger besetting not merely their cowslips, violets and dog-roses, but their very homes, with the groundwork of all their emotional and patriotic life, that they may grow up to fight such stupid iniquity to the uttermost?

There are lots of other things they need arousing to, nearer hand than these speculative atrocities. Just after passing through Weston village this low road meets at right angles the long highway, straight as an arrow, coming down from Bidford and Honeybourne, which I have previously referred to as marking the site of the old track way, Buckle Street, which we saw up on the hill. For 200-300 yards these roads are one, until the present highway turns off again at right angles to enter immediately the parish of Saintbury and pursue its way to Saintbury Cross. But Buckle Street goes straight forward to the hill, as the parish boundary, becoming from that point a wild green lane between two hedges overgrown with traveller's joy and blackberries. Where this begins there is, half buried in the grass, a little boundary stone, which many a year ago with Pickwickian eagerness I found to bear incised letters. However, it was no Roman altar. The letters turned out to consist of nothing more recondite than HERE ENDETH WESTON HIGHWAY. It is not for this I have mentioned it, but to record the fact that on travelling recently once more to look at this stone and the wild track passing up from it, I found the whole mouth of this lane in full sight of the highway positively choked with old pots, pans, hoops and other abominable refuse which had evidently been shot there regularly for some considerable time. This, then, is the latest use for this charming old lane, I suppose by the authorities, for such an accumulation;

such a miscellaneous assortment of rubbish could hardly have come together from any single private source. Unhappily such collections are too often met with in old quarries, woods or convenient hollows, and loathsome enough they are anywhere; but to see such a display there, in the broad day, flung in the mouth of little Buckle Street Lane to cheer the heart of every aesthetic wayfarer on the high road, I confess gave me a shock. Not only is this presented to the eyes of casual wayfarers in search of the picturesque, who pass this corner by the hundreds in every conceivable kind of vehicle, but there it stands as a perpetual object lesson to the children of the parishes who wander up this lane for its innumerable flowers, and I was going to say its birds' nests, but this is, of course, a thing of the past.

One really despairs of a good many things when this is possible. It is surely no extravagance to say that such a thing is nothing less than an outrage on the instinctive eye for beauty with which every little village child begins, and which only wants fostering properly to become a source of culture in itself, and of increasing joy to the end of life. It may be urged that the children will not notice the squalor. If so, then the harm is only the greater. Such a degradation of the wayside becomes a matter of course, and the way to all sorts of slovenly indifference to the natural fitness of things is opened. If there were nothing else in the parish, that little lane from here to the hilltop above Newcomb could alone supply an almost inexhaustible source of study and charm to the bright little souls born in its neighbourhood. Even in winter, when undoubtedly 'ways be foul' here, you get amply rewarded for wading through it. Were the days always spring or summer, and the ways always fair, we should miss perhaps the greater proportion of the beauty of the sky and landscape. For mere variety of cloud and colour, winter fairly beats them all, and the hues and gestures of winter herbage, dying and dead, are not to be surpassed. Even the highways hereabouts were always particularly rich in flowers, but these are getting rapidly trimmed away, so that one has to be especially grateful for any of these little forgotten tracks which have been left to do pretty much as they like.

Half a mile from this defiled end of Buckle Street Lane brings us to Saintbury Cross, at the foot of Saintbury village, as the church is at the other end at the top. A road turns off here, as at the other villages, and mounting the hill to Gunn's becomes that road we saw passing between Saintbury and Willersey quarries. This entrance to the village is open enough now, but some years ago it was overarched by great elm trees almost to the bottom. This shaded approach added a little picturesque mystery to the old clerk's village which accorded well with the last sparks of ancient life it then sheltered. Some dear old dame, like Mrs Smith herself, the clerk's wife, in her white sun-bonnet, would stop on the path as she met you and drop a gracious curtsey, which gave the keynote to all the rest you were to find as you went up the secluded slope. A woodpecker would cease tapping and eye you, then fly dipping away with long laugh. Possibly the loud whistle of a stormcock would ring along the hillside. As you got higher, beyond the first long archway of trees, you began to see it really was a village, especially if the little group of children had just come running out of school and were noisily playing in the road between the rectory gateway and the great chestnut tree by the path. If they were not there, and if by even better chance you heard in the silence the 'tap, tap' of a little hammer on the stones, you would quickly trace the sound to a figure sitting on a heap at the roadside by a small triangular slope of green, on which stood the chain and handle of the village well. Having settled that, you had only to go forward to that seated figure, note the courteous obeisance and the features raised to you as you stopped, and your introduction to the parish of old Saintbury would be complete.

ELEVEN

SAINTBURY

The admirable photograph by the late Mr Taunt preserves the old clerk on weekdays to the life. I have already stated that, in addition to being parish clerk and sexton, Mr William Smith was parish road-mender as well for a great number of years. His intelligence and share of early education enabled him to fulfil various other more private offices amongst his village neighbours. Music in every shape and form was his chief hobby, and this brought him into picturesque contact with many sides of parish life for several miles round. Of course, all his life he had been a ringer, and it was a touching sight in later days, when he was getting very old, to catch the bent, aged figure alone some Sunday morning in the belfry, when no other ringer had turned up, in the act of ringing three bells himself to summon the little congregation. He managed it by holding a rope in each hand and another looped for a foot to work it. Although rung thus with perfect regularity, I always fancied that I could tell from the fields when this was going on by the particularly piteous tone in which the three bells uttered their plaintive appeal of 'Oh, do come! Oh, do come!' which I must admit was once turned by an irreverent friend into 'Not for Joe! Not for Joe!'

The clerk was violin or bass viol in the church choir, until the degenerate harmonium and hymns took the place of the old instruments and anthems. Indeed, the clerk himself could take any one of the instruments most required, but the violin or bass viol was his habitual part. Even long after this practice had ceased as a regular thing, it was revived annually on the occasion of the harvest festival at Saintbury until the end of the century. The four customary instruments here were the bass viol, violin, flute and clarionet, In addition to all this the clerk was formerly in great request for servants' balls at the larger houses around, for musical evenings with friends, or any festivities, and of course he perambulated regularly for many years as violin with the waits at Christmas time, And in connection with these last the old man told me that it was a custom often to hire a non-player to go round with them to consume superfluous liquor, it not being etiquette to decline any offered. One champion in this line was known as Crutchy Ambleton, as under some infirmity he had always to use a crutch, but as the clerk said, he could drink 'a vast deal.' Only once was Crutchy known to have been overcome, when at some farmhouse they had been given 'cider like wine.' Crutchy had to get home as best he could, for he was unable to go farther.

The clerk wrote a beautiful hand also, and was good at accounts, so he was called upon to write many a letter for his illiterate neighbours, not excepting love letters, and he regularly made out various accounts, especially those of the estate woodman, who was Thomas Stanley in my time. Seeing that this career of his extended virtually through the whole of the nineteenth century, it is really deplorable that some systematic collection of the old clerk's experiences and memories was never made. I have already mentioned the circumstances under which he succeeded his grandfather in 1834 when only a boy of fourteen. He resigned the office in favour of his son Samuel on 3 January 1901, and left his native village soon after to live with a married daughter near Birmingham, under whose tender attention he passed in serenity his closing years. He did not die until 24 February 1910, in his ninetieth year, retaining his bright faculties virtually to the end, and was brought back to this beautiful green slope for his last resting place upon which all his real life had been passed. His career here fitly closed with the opening of the new century, for it was rapidly becoming a world he no longer knew, but of course it is impossible for the present writer ever to contemplate the singular beauty of that quiet spot apart from the genial spirit and picturesque figure that had imparted to it such vital charm. Still, I am again bound to admit that I could never discover in the old clerk himself any trace of sentimental or imaginative attachment to his home, such as I have found in old natives of Northumberland for instance. This certainly is going far for a contrast, especially as the imaginative temperament is well known to deepen as one goes towards the north. I suppose it is mainly a matter of race. The Angles of the north and the east were clearly of a more virile, or at least more imaginative stock than that of the Saxons which laid the ground work of this old district of Wiccesse. At all events, I lamented the deficiency in my old friend, though it possibly secured the absolute simplicity and naturalness which formed a great part of his charm. It was the knowledge of him and of the actual life there around him that gave such vivid comment on the most humorous parts of Shakespeare. Though I have wandered much and intimately through Warwickshire also, the atmosphere there never seemed to me to sustain the Shakespearean spirit so completely as these districts of Gloucestershire. It is to be remembered, too, that Shallow and his cousins Silence arid Slender are made Gloucestershire men. It is indeed evident that Shakespeare had been especially impressed by this Cotswold region, so there seems much to support the claim, not without other evidence too, that the poet had at some youthful impressionable period actually passed a good deal of time in this district, presumably during those dim years between his leaving Stratford and his appearance in London.

The picturesque figure and speech of the old clerk invariably suggested old Adam of *As You Like It*, a part which Shakespeare himself was traditionally said to have acted. And although the real forest of Arden is a few miles away in Warwickshire, the beautiful woodland glades of Saintbury coppice and Weston Park quite adequately sustained the sylvan atmosphere of that play. Indeed, at the foot of Saintbury coppice, running down the shaded crease that forms the New Coombe, was our best apology for:

The shallow rivers, to whose falls
Melodious birds sing madrigals.

Beds of roses and fragrant posies it certainly afforded in less questionable shape, for the poor little muddy stream was as gallantly decked out, from the first celandines, golden saxifrage and primroses, through the rosy and brambly year to the very last campion, St John's wort, bell-flower and old man's beard, as if it had been the most sparkling beauty in the world. Although many an antique root peeped out upon this brook it could not be said to brawl along the wood, for its voice was sweet and gentle, and even when swollen with melting snow or rain it only deepened its tone to a gurgling swoop. Nonetheless, the melancholy Jaques could have no difficulty in finding his thousand similes without the aid of any poor sequestered stag. Squirrels, stoats and voles were there, and very often a fox. A jay or two would always scold you, a magpie chuckle, woodpigeon croon, and hawk give his little scream as if mocking that of his victim. Then that haze of bluebells amongst the trees, shot by the May sun, as you sat under a big thorn to watch the throbbing throat of the nightingale as he flung his amazing snatches over you or drew out his long repeated note of agonising sweetness. Those things fortunately never leave you, and the very thought of them brings back the scented breath of the wood and the gentle voice of the water as if still about you.

Such was the bottom of Saintbury coppice, for it occupies the whole of one steep side of the little coomb, which as most readers will know is a valley with a mouth only, gaping from a hillside, and losing itself gradually up the slope. The old track of Buckle Street runs up the other side, at the top of which stands Newcomb House, and this side is more open, though the lower part is well sprinkled with self-sown brushwood. The very top of the crease ends just between Gunn's cottages and the house, so you look down and over it to the great Evesham vale from that road leading to the Narrows and Dover's Hill, of which I spoke before. I never think about that upper part of the coomb without being reminded of the singular fitfulness in the display of wild flowers. Never take a friend to see any startling show which delighted you the year before. You will be overwhelmed with disappointment and astonishment, and he or she may possibly, like Mr Pickwick, accuse you of being a humbug. Cowslip and purple orchis are common enough about here, but needless to say that both are lovely flowers, and when the two are intermingled in plenty over the surface of a meadow it is a sight not easily to be forgotten. The late W.H. Hudson used to tell us to do our utmost to catch sight of each bird 'at its best,' that is in some most charming or characteristic action or habit under some peculiarly favourable light, so that our minds may be stored with lovely visions which raise the whole of bird life to a very wonderful level. We should do just the same with wild flowers, if we really wish to love and cherish them as a source of undying inspiration to the end. So far, then, as cowslips and purple orchises in combination are concerned, I once caught them very distinctly at their best in a sloping meadow at the head of that coomb one spring in the early 1890s. It is that field, in the angle below the two roads, dropping down immediately behind the cottages, and is called Gunn's meadow. The whole surface of it that May was a carpet of those two flowers closely and evenly intermingled in the brilliantly green grass. I do not by any means ask for a mass of bloom to produce the effect I wish for, but in that particular instance it was undoubtedly the great expanse so favourably mixed that impressed me. Well, I had the opportunity of going for several successive springs to look for a repetition of this sight, but never again found it, nor anything approaching such a display. I could never learn that the meadow had received any particular treatment to affect its growth. Some years, of course, mere grazing had interfered with it, but by no means all. So it is obviously just some subtle combination of natural conditions that promotes or retards the blooming faculties of plants. It is only now and then that these influences unite to impel the vegetable tissues to put forth all their powers, exactly as some other mysterious combination occurs in the atmosphere to produce some rare and phenomenal glories of sunrise or sunset.

But apart from any exceptional displays, the mere average annual tribute of flowers in this district is wonderful enough. Their destruction on the highways I have referred to, but elsewhere every lane, wood and meadow is still full of those choicest old gems that appeal to every lover of the pure landscape. We need not trouble about rareties. Some of the commonest are, happily, some of the most beautiful. Violets, king-cups, lady's-smock; blue milkwort, fairy-flax and yellow-rattle; codlins-and-cream, meadow-sweet and rose-bay; hare bell, tormentil and wild thyme. Who would ask for more? Yet these are not a hundredth part of what every half-mile will in their different seasons offer. I hardly dare go into Saintbury coppice again for fear of spending all the rest of my pages there. But I can not pass from it without a glance at that rugged track which goes up one side of it, on leaving Buckle Street by the brook at the bottom, to join the regular hill road from Saintbury village at the top. Most of it lies between the wood and the great hedgerow of one of the rector glebe fields, but although thus hemmed in as a trackway, it is itself almost entirely overgrown with tall bracken and brushwood, so as to become simply a narrow wilderness up the hillside. The tangle is bound together by honey suckle, roses, blackberries, bryony, clematis, great pink vetch, and I know not what, whilst the squirrels scuttle in the branches overhead and throw down the flakes of the larch cones upon you as they nibble them to pieces. I always felt this to be the very heart of Saintbury parish, and life can offer few ampler compensations than that of having allowed you to sit here soon after sunrise on those 29 May mornings in the late 1880s and early 1890s to await the breaking forth of the church bells at six o'clock. For actually until that late date did the custom of ringing in Restoration Day survive in this remote parish.

But historical and natural charm go together here to perfection. As soon as one looks at all closely into it, it becomes surprising to find what there is yet to be done historically for every parish in the land, in spite of the cartloads of books already issued upon such a subject. Even here, nearly the whole of our social life might be traced and illustrated from the very beginning out of the parish soil. Ancient mound and camp crown the hilltop, the latter no doubt an outpost of the large one on the adjoining Willersey Hill. Some have connected the camp with the Danes and explained the name of the place as Sweyn's bury. But no doubt such a position went back as a fortification far beyond that. The name, I suppose, may be as claimed, for in the *Domesday Book* it is spelt 'Suineberie'; then in 1349 'Seynesbury'; in the second year of Edward VI, 'Seynburie'; and by the fifth year of James I the 't' has got in, thus 'Seyntburye alias Senburye'. So it is not from any peculiar sanctity that the spot acquired the present suggestive form of its name. In the *Domesday Book* the king retained the lordship, but the knight's fee was in the Musards of Miserden until the reign of Edward I, when the manor and impropriation of the church went to Evesham Abbey. To the Musards then must be credited the church with its Norman doorways and later broach spire. There was a chantry, too, established at some time in the little church, no doubt in the south transept which is the present belfry, as the piscina is still in the wall there. This, no doubt, would also go back to the time before the possession by Evesham Abbey, for I suppose they generally had in view the weal of the founder's soul, however liberally worded. 'A man might make a chantry,' says Burn's *Ecclesiastical Law*, 'by licence of the king, without the ordinary; for the ordinary hath nothing to do therewith. The main use and intent of these chantries was, for prayers for souls departed, on a supposition of purgatory, and of being released from thence by masses satisfactory. These chantries were dissolved by the statute of the 1st Ed. VI. cap. 14.' Amongst the certificates made at the time of this dissolution is an interesting one relating to this chantry at Saintbury:

Seynburie P'oche.
Lande given to ffind a lampe there. The
yerely value thereof ... xiid. the whole
Distributed to the poor ever sithens lampes
taken down ... xiid.

Evesham Abbey retained possession until the Dissolution, upon which the manor and two mills were granted to Richard Bartlet, and this family held the property for several generations, until they disposed of it to Sir Hugh Brawne. It is interesting to note that, in the hands of Evesham Abbey, the one mill of the Domesday Survey had become two. The one in the *Domesday Book* had the distinction of being the mill of least value recorded in the county of Gloucester, namely sixpence annually. Both mills must have long since disappeared, but the site of one, or probably both, is still clearly shown by the great semicircular mound enclosing the mill race which remains in the field where the brook runs beside the low road. This field bears the name of Naits Ground, as I was informed by the old clerk, and though he spelt the name thus for me, he said they always called and pronounced it 'The Nites.'

But this devolution of manors, advowsons and other property is, of course, the mere dry-as-dust of parish history unless woven in with the daily social life of the successive inhabitants, which alone gives interest and charm to the story by associating it with the natural features of the landscape. To know anything of the dramatic interest attached to every two or three generations of common life, even in a remote little parish like this, one must catch the old clerk (who was sexton also) digging a grave, or in the belfry, if not engaged upon the roads; the woodman cutting the coppice, or sowing his bag of haws and ash keys in the linch bank nursery; the hedge-carpenter buried in the wood at his fragrant work of splitting the ash and withy poles for gates and hurdles; the shepherd taking hay to his sheep in the snow on the hill; to say nothing of the rickyard, the orchard and cider mill, and the numberless opportunities of the housewives' firesides. Certainly one has to look a little bit farther nowadays in the villages for this kind of thing, but it may be found still, though it is easy to see that the form of its being presented will become very different to the later generation. Just as rhyme and metre seem to be no longer attributes of what we used to call poetry, so to the sentimental observer country life is getting rapidly shorn of most of its graces and seems to be doing its best to assimilate itself to prose. Still, I suppose there is no philosophical reason why the prose of one generation should not appear poetry to the next and *vice versa*, if each has a mind to think it so.

As I have no present intention of going farther into the detailed history of Saintbury, I have not sought out how and when the open fields in the parish were enclosed. There is no mention of an Enclosure Act in the standard reference books of the county, but that some part was open until about the eighteenth century seems to be suggested by the remark in Rudder's *New History* (1779) when speaking of the church property that 'a piece of ground is assigned to the minister in satisfaction for enclosures.' Whilst in 1608, when Sir Hugh Brawne bought the manor, there was included in his conveyance 'common of pasture for all kinds of cattle in Seyntburye,' with free warren, view of frankpledge, and advowson of the church. The enclosures immediately about the village seem to be old both by name and appearance. The names of the fields are delightful, such as Court Ground, Long Croft, Godwell, Tundish, Ram Close, Church Close, Coney Green, and Castle Hill or Round Hills, where the camp is. Two at the very top are peculiarly interesting, namely Hangman's Close and Hunt's Hill, as the clerk wrote it, but said it was commonly pronounced 'Untsills.

Of Hangman's Close he could say no more, but such a name seems to take it back to quite a remote time of manorial rights. 'Untsills, he suggested, might be Hounds' Hill, for a pack of hounds was long ago kept at New Coombe, the ruined buildings of the kennels having stood there until quite recently. But my pretty obvious proposal was for 'Unts (or Wants') Hill, the word 'want', for a mole, being invariably pronounced "unt' hereabouts, and the soil of that field was much frequented by moles. How the word 'unt may readily and naturally be taken for hunt by anybody not familiar with the local dialect is shown in the 1in ordnance map of the district, where a remote farm on the hill between Cleeve Cloud and Belas Knap was recorded by the old surveyors as Huntley Farm, but which is corrected in later issues to the proper form of Wantley. The objection to a 'w' in the older vernacular here, amounting almost to an inability to use the letter, is very pronounced. Woodman is always 'oodman, won't (will not) is 'unt, woman is 'oman, and so on. Even the old clerk, who had friends at Wootton Wawen in Warwickshire, always spoke of the place as 'Ootton 'Awen, But that this arises from no physical disability is shown by the use of the word 'whatever', which like 'however' turns up on every occasion. 'Ur 'ouldn't go whatever,' would be the natural way of expressing emphatically a man, woman or child's refusal to take any particular situation.

But to return to the enclosure of the open fields, no doubt the lands affected in later times would be those situated at the two extremities of the parish. The upper part we saw when I was rambling on the hilltop. The lower part is that skirting the vale beyond the cross and the low road by Lower Field Lane. It extends about a couple of miles from the village, widening out to touch the parishes of Bretforton and Honeybourne to the north. The farm known as Saintbury Grounds embraces a considerable portion of this. The three acres which formed part of the endowment of the Saintbury clerkship appeared a relic of the open field system, for they were situated in the midst of the ground which appertained to the Saintbury Cross Farm on this lower level part of the parish just below the cross. The clerk's property was not fenced off at all, but was merely marked out of the field by a narrow strip of grass about a foot wide called a mere, as was such a boundary in the old common field system. The inconvenience of this had evidently long been felt, at any rate by the tenants of the farm, for the clerk told me various efforts had been made to induce him to change his allotment for another tract nearer home, but nothing would persuade him that the transaction was free from jugglery, and no persuasion or threat could ever move him. As he said with his shrewd smile, 'Possession is nine points of the law,' and he intended to hand down the clerk's endowment to any successor as he had received it. Lawyers had, at one time, evidently been consulted, for the old man, not without some pride, affirmed that his property had been declared 'an ancient demiscene,' – that is how he always pronounced it – although there was no sort of title deed, nor could any trace of the original grant be found. But it was as much a freehold as the parson's rectory and glebe, and held upon precisely the same terms of prescriptive right. In addition to these acres, a cottage with garden and orchard in the middle of the village was also appurtenant to the clerkship, so it is obvious enough if Mr Smith had been in the least degree commercially minded, the acquisition of such a snug little freehold at the age of fourteen might have carried him on to the rank of farmer very easily in the course of such a long life. No ambition of the kind had ever stirred him. Indeed, he seemed to have some moral suspicion of any such advancement, for of one man who had 'got on' from very small beginnings he would give sinister hints as to his methods, and declare solemnly in his deep voice that, after all, 'it was a black day at the last.' For his own part, Providence had sustained him through many trials and would do so, he had no doubt, to the end. Self-righteous my old friend certainly never was, but one could not repress a smile when, after relating some act of meanness or petty imposition on the part of somebody against himself, he would complacently conclude with 'somehow things didn't prosper with' the culprit. There was much else to show that the old clerk fully shared the opinion of the son of Sirach that 'sin sticketh between buying and selling,' and that commercial prosperity was only to be had by nefarious means.

His music sufficed for everything beyond the mere needs of subsistence and indeed ministered very materially to them also. Any record of his career in this line alone would have been of the greatest interest, associated as it necessarily was with so much of the village comedy. One would like to know more of his fellow musicians, of whom there seems to have been plenty. A former parish constable, for instance, whom the clerk called 'Old Turner' and pronounced 'a most excellent good musician,' was one, whose date I forget. This man's primitive lock-up was a kind of wood and coal shed at the back of the house, known expressively as 'the hole.' When the clerk looked in, there would be immediately much music, in the midst of which Mrs Turner would remark, to remind her husband of professional duty, 'There be a man in the hole.'

'Ay,' replied the constable, 'but I've locked the door, missus. We'll have another tune.'

Later on, Turner was unable to play (it had been usually the trombone), 'as he had had his teeth knocked down his throat,' calmly explained the old clerk.

The changes in the social life of this little village must be fully equalled by alterations in its external appearance. The loss of the two mills long ago has been referred to. How so many dwelling-houses and cottages come to have disappeared is not so easily explained. According to the statements of Sir Richard Atkyns, 1712, and Rudder in his *New History*, 1779, no less than twenty-three houses had gone entirely in the course of those sixty years. Atkyns gives the number of houses in the parish as fifty-four, with about 240 inhabitants, ten of whom were freeholders. Rudder gives the number of houses in his time as thirty-one, and the people as having decreased to 135. Such a downfall, I am afraid, points to the effect of enclosure and a consequent increase in the size of farms, a process which has evidently continued, for the number of inhabitants by now has got down to less than 100.

Although the population diminished so materially during the eighteenth century, a newcomer or two at the same time found their way thither, for it was the old clerk's paternal grandfather who first settled at Saintbury. He was George Smith, and came from Bidford. But having been apprenticed to a weaver at Honeybourne, just half-way between the two villages, something drew him a step farther along Buckle Street towards the hill. Of the clerk's maternal grandfather and predecessor in the clerkship, William Newman, I have spoken in a previous chapter, and to his own sweet old wife I have made a still more shadowy reference. But through the latter I got many a glimpse into their earlier married life, and although her large family had grown up and dispersed before my intimacy with Saintbury, it was easily to be seen that the old soldier's daughter had throughout shed a brave and gracious influence over her home. Amongst other interesting glimpses of his military father-in-law, the old clerk gave one of his early life when stationed with the guard over Napoleon at St Helena, the soldier having proudly handed down to eager listeners the fact that one day, when on duty, the ex-emperor stopped and eyed him with the words: 'My man, if all my soldiers had been like you I should not have been here.' I suppose Bonaparte could speak English; I never heard that the Gloucestershire private could speak or understand French. At all events I hand on the story as it was given to me.

TWELVE

WILLERSEY

Barely a mile from Saintbury Cross along the low road stands the next village of Willersey. Not only is it a larger village, but it is altogether of a different type. It gathers round a goodly green, and offers many other features of Gloucestershire life not presented by its little neighbour. The main road passes zigzag right through the village, and not a single house is allowed to stray up the hillside, or at least was not until the last few years. But in the writer's mind these two parishes from long familiarity became one, supplementing from each other whatever might be lacking to either. It is in no sense derogatory to the life of Willersey to say that it did not ever produce a counterpart to the old clerk of Saintbury, for on all hands that figure was admittedly unique. But, of course, in mere variety of local character, Willersey was very far ahead. So interesting was it in that respect and so diverse that I shall not attempt here more than the most superficial glance at that aspect of the village life. It must be remembered, too, that all I say is in retrospect, and may probably bear not the slightest resemblance to the later developments of the present century. Besides, except in actual features or matters of fact, I do not attempt to separate these two neighbouring parishes. Dialect, general habits of life and so on, are very much the same in all these lower road villages, and in dwelling upon one I shall no doubt recall impressions gathered elsewhere.

In fact, now in leaving Saintbury, it seems too bad to have made no special reference to that charming bit at the foot of the village where the old cross stands at the meeting of the four roads. It is undoubtedly one of the most beautiful peeps of our old landscape which this lower road affords. The venerable cross itself, dating from about the fifteenth century, had, of course, been mutilated, and the piety or genius of the eighteenth or early nineteenth century had hit upon the idea of embellishing the decapitated shaft with a painted pineapple at the top. As stated by Mr Pooley in his *Notes on the Crosses of Gloucestershire* (1868), this was replaced by the present dial and Maltese cross 'about twenty years ago.' All the rest of it, however, including the four steps, is original, and it may be supposed played some part possibly in gaining the village the present form of its name. Mr Pooley says that the cross is supposed to have been the resting place for the funeral procession before it started up the hill to the church. And no doubt it would serve well for that purpose, as the mills and several of the lost houses were situated beside that lower road, but it is not likely that that would be the primary object of its erection. We know what a common practice it was with our pious forefathers to erect such crosses by the roadside and in villages for general devotional purposes. We saw one up at the hill village of Condicote, and of course this district as elsewhere affords many more of varying degrees of beauty and interest.

Saintbury Church, too, up at the top of the village on that green slope just below the steep Castle Bank, is quite as tempting, but so is every cottage and farmhouse, field and hedgerow, for a matter of that. Still, as the rambling nature of these pages has already shown, I did not mean to confine myself to much detail of any particular locality, so I will escape from Saintbury with a closing reference to the church bells. There is such an individuality, I mean personality, about them, together with those in the tower at Willersey, which is so blended with the sun and clouds, birds and flowers of that radiant hillside as to demand at least as definite and grateful a recognition of one as of the other. I spoke at the outset of my original introduction to the actual presence of the Saintbury bells in the steeple on my first encountering the old clerk. I often went up to them afterwards, but of course it was in their voices that all their personal charm and influence lay. It seems instinctive to attribute this personality to church bells, for not only so many popular rhymes chronicle their supposed sentiments, but the old bell founders also usually inscribed them with words in their proper person. There are six of these bells at Saintbury, and although the first one bears date the year after William Smith's election to the clerkship, I never asked him if he remembered anything about it. The inscriptions are as follow:

1. I Rudhall fect. 1835.
2. Henry Bagley made mee 1678.
3. Henry Bagley of Chacombe 1678.
4. Henricus Bagley me fecit 1678.
5. Henry Bagley made mee 1678.
6. John Freeman and William Hobbs Churchwardens 1678.

No doubt there must have been bells here before these late dates, which probably chronicle re-casting only, but I am not aware that there is any record of the transactions in parish accounts or elsewhere. Churchwarden Freeman, at all events, has left his name in the parish soil as well as on the bells, for 'Freeman's Orchard' still stands in the village below Church Close.

From near here also are two field paths leading to Willersey. One of them turns down the sloping grounds and, after crossing, two or three big meadows brings you to the field called Marbrook, over the stile of which you enter Willersey parish, and so to the church and churchyard, through the latter of which the path comes to Church Lane midway in the village. The other path from Saintbury, which is safer in wet weather, leads from the beautiful old cherry orchard below the church (where Cherry Wake Sunday used to be held in former days), right across Ram Close, Gibbs's Meadow and Stanthill, otherwise Hopyard Meadow, to the main road descending Willersey Bank. This reaches the village at the corner by the Top Farm. Although in the preceding pages I have been in fancy approaching Willersey by the low road, I rather think the best way to come to this, as to the rest of these villages, is to drop upon it by this road from the hill. To be sure, like so much else, not only is the road itself materially altered, but there is no longer that beautiful old gabled Top Farm, with its old brown and white spaniel lying on its own little bit of green at the corner, there at all to greet you. The house was removed bodily some years ago to form the nucleus of a larger residence a little way up the hill, and the village corner is now blinded by a long 12ft wall. The other private house opposite, where Mrs Halford for so many years kept her school, has been entirely reconstructed and enlarged, whilst, as I write, another old farmhouse of that corner group with its quaint projecting upper storey has had to be entirely demolished and rebuilt, as it was no longer safe.

So only memory can now recall the homely charm of that entrance to Willersey as it appeared forty, nay down to twenty years ago. But I have no intention of lamenting inevitable change. I have said enough, perhaps too much of this in earlier pages. In dwelling upon the old village I only wish to recall some aspects of its former life which surely have a perennial charm by sheer force of their simplicity, the loss of which in the later stress of rural life we all profess to deplore. The change in the hill road is not all due to this later progress. What we call nature began it, when one August morning in the 1890s, after a ferocious gale, I took my early walk towards the sun to find that road blocked right up to the Saintbury footpath by half a dozen huge elm trees flung by the wind across it. That road, like the other entrances to the village, used to be overarched by magnificent trees, under which in the spring, amongst other things, you could listen to that extraordinary vibrating tap of the woodpecker, which always seems to me one of the most astonishing of bird sounds. His heavy blows are intelligible enough, but those quivering taps given with such rapidity as to make one continuous ghost of a rattle seem as mysterious as the weird drumming of the snipe. Sometimes the movements are so blended in sound as to suggest even the croaking of a frog. The very thought of it brings back the whole of that glowing hillside early on a spring morning. The sun would dazzle you now and then in going up as it caught your eye between the trees from over the Saintbury green camp, dappling the whole road with shadows, and throwing great shafts of light before you where the trunks and branches were loose enough to allow it. If some particularly sparkling diamond struck you in the hedge bottom, trace it, and ten to one it would be a bead of moisture in the very eye of a violet just at the proper angle with the sun. Chiffchaff and willow wren, thrush and blackbird were evidently as ecstatic as yourself, and very often the nightingale in the little coppice on the right would thrill you with some notes carried over from midnight. When this last bird sleeps I do not know, but its repose must be taken in snatches, unless they arrange to relieve one another, for during the spring at any hour of the day or night you may hear its song. But those are notes of pure song, and do not seem the result of alarm. The bird of all others which is the most warily watchful seems to be the poor persecuted peewit, with his sweet plaintive cry which you would think might disarm even a fox. But they, I suppose, do actually appoint sentinels, though this can only be done during the period of flocking. Yet throughout the nesting time also, if you pass along a country road at any hour of the night, or put your head out of the window when yourself wakeful, the peewit's plaint is sure to break the silence and proclaim that he is as wakeful, if unhappily more nervous than you are.

That road never really recovered from that August gale. Soon afterwards nearly all the remaining trees of any size were felled, and other changes rapidly swept in which carried away most of its earlier attractions. It even rose to the dignity, I believe, of motorcycle races up its perilous ascent, so no doubt willow wren and nightingale will have had to slink quietly away to more secluded quarters, although it must be confessed that neither of these precious birds is at all shy. But like the uncertainty in flowers which I have mentioned, you can never be sure either of finding birds where you expected.

This mere natural fluctuation of birds in various districts, without any obvious human interference, is a curious problem of which I cannot feel that any satisfactory explanation has yet been offered. Surely the food problem is not quite enough. One such inexplicable desertion at Willersey that I especially lamented was on the part of the redstart, that winsome personality and songster, so suggestive of sunshine, apple blossom and an old orchard or garden wall. Through the early 1890s he had seemed a very part of the especially radiant sunshine of those years. Though his song is no more than a sweet beginning, and never gets to what it seems to promise, yet few songs take so great a hold of you, and in the present writer's mind the redstart's fragment takes a place even with the inimitable achievement of the little willow wren from whom you can never dissociate the magical words:

> That strain again! It had a dying fall:
> O, it came o'er my ear like the sweet sound
> That breathes upon a bank of violets,
> Stealing and giving odour!

That the loss of the redstart was from no purely local cause and was pretty widespread, is shown by the fact that the late Mr Warde Fowler lamented a similar diminution of the same bird about the same time at Kingham, in his volume on that north Oxfordshire parish.

Willersey and Saintbury were particularly rich in birds of all sorts, for there was no game preserving in either parish. The characteristic sound of the hillside during most of the year is the joyous laugh of the green woodpecker or hicwell, called also in some parts here the stock eagle, by obvious corruption of hick'ell. Magpies, jays, owls, sparrow-hawks and kestrels with all the rest classed as vermin were allowed a free hand, and so added their contribution to the charms of the landscape. The magpie is certainly a beautiful creature, but he needs every bit of it if we are to condone his atrocities. I am not quite sure of my feelings about him after watching him assiduously work the whole hedge of a field, with that ironical chuckle as he progresses, and then on following in his track find the fresh thrushes', blackbirds' and even dicky dunnocks' eggs with his angular beak mark in the sides of them strewn along the grass. From the orchards and farmyards he steals a great number of tiny chickens also. But I was a little astonished once to find that he did not disdain even such quarry as the house sparrow. At a cottage where I was sleeping I was awakened one spring morning between four and five by a great uproar amongst the sparrows who had their nests in the eaves above my open window. An acacia tree stood close by, nearly touching the house, and almost as soon as I was awake to the sparrows' clatter I became conscious also of its cause. The magpie's chuckle explained all, and, jumping out to look, there in the branches close by I saw a crowd of sparrows scolding the assailant, who evidently had designs on their nests in the eaves, but who on seeing my head emerge gave a final chuckle and went off to try elsewhere. This probably explained the callow young, the eggs and even whole nests of the sparrows which were frequently found thrown down to the path below, and which I had put down to squabbling amongst the rival sparrows themselves. But one has to get over these vexing aspects of natural things, as I believe I have remarked before. It is the law of life, and we must accustom ourselves to taking a rational interest in the fray.

But I was trapped into these remarks about birds by the changes in that beautiful hillside. My original intention in this chapter was to give a glimpse of old Willersey as a whole. It is one of the compact villages clustered about a green, though this green itself has got somewhat divided. The bit in front of the Top Farm and the adjoining row of cottages where the hill road comes in is parted from the main central portion, where most of the wake is held and which is itself divided by the main road passing through. At the lower end, a further bit is separated from the large green by an island clump of cottages, thus allotting to the ancient Blue Bell Inn another little green of its own, beside which also the village smithy used to stand, where Church Lane turns aside to the rectory and church. The main road parts this green also from another opposite portion which is known as Sawpit Green, where long ago the sawpit and village pump used to be, and which adjoins the large duck pond standing directly in front of the beautiful old Pool Farm and so giving the latter its name. It is this farm, by the by, which bears a charge of £8 a year payable to the Penderell family by an old grant for having hidden King Charles in the oak after the battle of Worcester. Even below Sawpit Green and the pool is yet another and last strip of green, keeping the houses back from the road on that side and stretching down to the foot of the village where four roads meet. Thus is the whole village threaded by a broad green, the only real interruption being that island of cottages midway, not picturesque in itself, which I always felt I should have removed and built elsewhere if I had had the magic wand. That would really have been a desirable change.

Looking up from this lower end of the village, the hill immediately behind offers rather a bare appearance now, which was formerly so well wooded.

There were really several noble elms upon that slope, both of the common sort and the wych, for the two kinds flourish equally well here. A very fine wych elm still stands by the wall of the Saintbury churchyard, but it did not equal one which used to stand on the furzy hillside below Willersey camp and which some children I knew delighted in and named it the Swinging Tree. The wych elm does not tower up erect and throw his head out in fine clouds at the top of a tall trunk, leaving merely 'brushwood sheaf' round the bole, but he spreads out great boughs from the very beginning which are diffused upwards like a fountain, and fall in a shower of pendulous branches and twigs covering a very large area in a free space. The Swinging Tree had full scope for his powers, and had surrounded his trunk with three or four enormous boughs which made a graceful swoop as if to touch the grass, but, when a few feet from it, turning outwards and upwards to the sun, so as to open into twigs and blend their leaves with the upper branches. To some of these you had to jump as to a trapeze and swing by the hands merely. But there was one long bough whose lowest curve midway came within 3ft of the ground, free from twigs until the outer branches. Here was an ideal saddle for several children at a time, one behind the other, without their feet touching the ground, so if you could get an elder to pull the end branches and sway the whole bough up and down with gradually increasing vigour it became merely a question of who tired first. And down below there lay the village, with perhaps that remarkable wake music coming up fitfully on the June breeze, or filling the heavy thundery air with its blatant drone. Not that I mean for a moment to depreciate Willersey wake even in its music. There was a zest and exhilaration about this village spectacle which even Robert Dover would have approved, with a smile possibly of compassion for such degenerate descendants. Of that function, however, I will say a little more presently. I am now thinking of that scroll of the parish as a whole, unrolled as it were from the hilltop, and flowing out into the vale, side by side with its neighbour Saintbury. In size and shape the parishes are very much the same, what I have called little Saintbury being even a 100-200 acres the larger. But Willersey is open to the world. Even before the village lost its trees there was none of the snug seclusion of Weston or Aston Subedge about it. Its name suggests something in the nature of an island amidst swampy lands, as does Badsey also, the parish next to Willersey towards the River Avon at Evesham. Those lower fields can be swampy enough still in wet wintry weather, and the little brook which meanders through them, the same which rises by Saintbury coppice and turned the Saintbury mill-wheels, is often in doubt as to which way the slope lies. But in spring and summer they were as lovely as any our landscape affords.

We could go all the four miles to Honeybourne station by a delightful path through these level fields, only passing the farm houses of Saintbury and Honeybourne Grounds on the way. It was our nearest station in those days, and if you arrived by an evening train to walk home, those silent fields with the green hills behind, all golden in the sunset and barred with long shadows, came as a wonderful benediction. Silent enough they seemed as you listened to your train speeding away in the distance, but it was a silence emphasised by all manner of bird and farm sounds. The thrush and blackbird never attained more sublime heights than there, and of the tree-pipit, which seems an inseparable part of that little avenue beside Saintbury Grounds, it is hardly safe to speak. That bird affects listeners in various ways. For me it almost reaches the poignancy suggested by Burns in his address to it under the name of woodlark, for no doubt this is the bird he intended, as it is very generally called the woodlark, and the real woodlark is, I believe, virtually not found in Scotland. Though he begins with an appeal to the 'soothing fond complaining':

> Again, again that tender part,
> That I may catch thy melting art,

it becomes too much for him before the bird reaches the tree again.

> For pity's sake, sweet bird, nae mair!
> Or my poor heart is broken.

The whole action attending the song no doubt adds much to its effect. It is surely one of the most captivating of all bird movements. Starting from its twig, there is the silent fling up into the air above the tree-top without a note, then with the gradual gliding descent, the little wings outstretched motionless, both voice and gesture blend in tender supplication as that first rippling gush of song melts into the repeated note of inimitable appeal when the bird is nearing its perch on the tree again. This attains a point of dramatic completeness which is quite irresistible.

Skylarks, peewits and partridges, of course, loved these fields too, and it is hardly necessary to add that if you were crossing them in the dusk, when little white moths were about your footsteps, and cockchafers, otherwise maybees, booming past your ear or smacking your face, the fine halloo of the owls would ring across the meadows from every direction. In one particular hedgerow (not the one by the brook) the nightingale hardly ever failed you. It is years since I walked those meadows and cornlands, but I hope all these things are still there. No doubt these lands were open and common fields until the Enclosure Act for this parish was passed in 1767. If one thinks of it, the changes in the life and landscape wrought by these acts must have been a moving experience for the simple inhabitants of the rural parishes, beyond the mere material injury to most of them. Disaffection and even riots we hear of in places, but I have not learned that there was anything of this sort in Willersey. The whole routine of life must have been shattered for many, and the general effect upon the actual villagers far more radical than that wrought even by the dissolution of the monasteries.

In the *Domesday Book* this 'Willersei' manor was in the hundred of 'Wideles', one of those I mentioned before as having been ultimately merged in the larger Kiftsgate, and though we have long since passed the time of guess work in etymology, I wondered whether these wide leas over which I wandered had helped to give this name to the hundred. There were certainly some difficulties in the way, for the termination *ley* is, I believe, strictly an open glade in a wood, and had that been the nature of this locality one would have expected that suffix in the name 'Willersey' also, instead of the island suggestion. But (except on the lamps of the new railway halt) the 'l' was never admitted to this latter word. There is *Domesday*, as stated, and long before that we have, from the Saxon charters, 'Willerseia', A.D. 709, and 'Wyllereseie' or 'Wyllersege' in 850, at which early date the place was already the property of Evesham Abbey. In view of this, I take it, later corruptions such as 'Wyllardseye' need not be taken into consideration. The abbey retained this manor down to the Dissolution, and the abbot of Evesham seems to have had some residential connection with the place, for in the meadow still called Church Close, at the end farthest from the church, is a hollow claimed to have been the site of that dignitary's fishpond. In that field also used to be a very noble elm tree, which, to sustain the association, some of us called the Abbot's Elm, although, of course, the tree could by no means claim any such age or distinction. This field, with the view from it up to Saintbury Church and the hillside generally, is perhaps the most beautiful the parish affords, and for gracious English landscape could hardly be excelled elsewhere, although I have deprecated from the outset this foolish trick of comparison.

THIRTEEN

ROUND THE GREEN

Enough has been said of the hill portion of Willersey parish where the camp and quarry lie. The descent from there to the village is even more abrupt than that to the other villages I have mentioned, so on this account it never became a general channel of communication between the vale and the uplands as did the roads over Broadway, Aston and other of these hills. The hilltop here is only 6–7ft below the 900, so the drop to the village almost in a direct line is more than 600ft. Saintbury Church is on a little terrace running along the hillside whose level is about midway between the two, and it was just above this line, going in the other direction, that the Swinging Tree lay. There was a delightful path all along it to Collier's Knap, whence you dropped into Broadway, and this was the usual way taken to that village by the old clerk when he went for music with his friends there. Yet I could never find that my old friend paid the slightest heed either to the landscape spread out before him towards Bredon Hill and the Malverns, or to the inexhaustible interests of the immediate path. Indeed, in the real countryman, when otherwise of marked intelligence, there seems a peculiar talent for absolute vacancy. It is just an extension of that faculty on which even no less a man than Wordsworth prided himself in those words of 'Personal Talk':

> Better than such discourse doth silence long,
> Long, barren silence, square with my desire;

To sit without emotion, hope, or aim,
In the loved presence of my cottage fire,
And listen to the flapping of the flame,
Or kettle whispering its faint undersong.

That this has been one of nature's primal blessings to the countryman nobody will deny, since it offers in itself an impenetrable armour to shafts which, under certain conditions of his life, would deal death-thrusts to any degree of sensibility. Unfortunately, this armour is being rapidly stripped from simple souls without anything effectual being given in its place. This is the danger for country folk. Call the old thing insensibility if we like, but it was at least compatible with the virtue of consummate heroism in the face of tribulation and death. It did not extend to moral inertia. No wider play of self-sacrifice, of mutual help in time of trouble, was ever known to the highest culture than that which formed an instinctive part in the lives of these ten-shilling-a-week illiterate peasants. I remember well the tone in which the old clerk would testify to this quality in somebody we might be speaking about with the words 'he or she was there in the day of trial.' Nobody at all acquainted with rural life today will dispute the slackening of these strong but simple virtues on all hands. We try to hope that this is more than compensated by official doles and 'a higher standard of living.' But that old quality was most assuredly twice-blessed, and its disappearance can hardly be balanced by shrewd calculations how to cheat the exchequer, or by the acquisition in times of boom of canned peaches and tan shoes.

Willersey must for a very long time have represented just these simplest elements of rural life, the very life blood of the nation. The rectory, three or four substantial homesteads, two or three craftsmen and tradesmen, a couple of inns, and, for a time last century at all events, a lawyer and horse doctor. The rest were just the shepherds', the carters' and the labourers' cottages. There does not seem ever to have been a squire or other predominant family, nor does any existing residence suggest it. Nobody intimate with country life for the last generation or two can ever cease to lament what is nothing less than the end of the country squire. The crass stupidity of the insidious but too successful warfare carried on against this race by the paramount industrial spirit can only be fully realised by those who see, in the sentiment of rural life, a positive genius of its own essential to the health of any community fit to be called a state. But it is not my object to enlarge on that here. From the fact of Willersey having had no squire, I only meant to say that the dramatic variety and interest of country life was undoubtedly widened by some villages having grown up under these conditions. Indeed, an extremely interesting study in comparative English village life could be supplied by a candid and impartial review of the later history and social development of two rural parishes in the same neighbourhood from this point of view – one that had been squire-ridden, as the cant phrase is, and one that had been for many generations free to work out its own salvation. I am not aware of its having been attempted in a strictly historical spirit, with an imaginative grasp of the whole of life and free from all special pleading on either side. Candour would, of course, also be required in the selection of the types, for we are all familiar enough with the failings of individual squires, as we may also be with the exceptional barbarity of certain free villages.

Willersey, I fancy, would afford an excellent example of the unsquired parish. Its life must have been typically placid, independent and picturesque. Like all these villages nestling on and under the slope, in architecture and material it partakes of the character of the hill more than of the vale. All the houses are of stone, and with the exception of a few thatched they are roofed with the same. Several of them afford extremely beautiful details of the true Cotswold type, but I must lament once more the loss of that top corner which up to a few years ago grouped the chief of them and equalled any of its neighbours in characteristic charm. With it went, for Willersey, the last strain of an old song, that song which seemed to echo in the very stones before you as you came from the hill and for which they so pathetically called.

> O, fellow! come, the song we had last night.
> Mark it, Cesario, it is old and plain:
> The spinsters and the knitters in the sun,
> And the free maids that weave their thread with bones,
> Do use to chant it: it is silly sooth,
> And dallies with the innocence of love
> Like the old age.

Beautiful the old stones were, but it must be admitted they sadly lacked the natural embroidery of cottage gardens. The very scheme of the houses did not allow it. It was a grievous deficiency in the village as a whole; I mean in the open, palpable village as you looked at it. There were, to be sure, some beautiful old gardens hidden away, but the little cottage gardens which suggest so much and which bring such colour and fragrance into the homely details of everyday life were entirely wanting to Willersey. Happily the garden and nurseries of my friend Mr John Andrews were and still are an open joy by the green there, and might seem embroidery enough for the whole parish. But the great value of a garden is in possession. Let it be ever so tiny, ever so poor a thing, but mine own. A few gillies, snapdragons, and sweet-williams, not merely to throw their fragrance to the passer-by, but to give a posy for the cottage table as well as for the jam jar on the green turf in the churchyard. In these little things we touch the very heart of country life, at a point, too, which has such an immeasurable influence on the children of the parish, upon whom the development of the place so largely depends.

As the manor was in the possession of Evesham Abbey for so many centuries, there must have been many interesting associations in that direction, but I am not aware that any trace of such influence has lingered in the village customs. Certainly, a curious piece of information, relative possibly to one of the Evesham abbots personally, was given me by my friend the Rev. Charles O. Bartlett, formerly for a good many years rector of Willersey, in the fact of his parish clerk having told him that many years ago, when a portion of the wall in the south transept of the church was being removed, he, the clerk, saw a skeleton embedded in the wall. Now, Abbot Brokehampton of Evesham is recorded to have built the chancels of five churches, of which Willersey was one, and to have been buried in the wall of the chancel of Willersey. The rector not unnaturally concluded that the skeleton exposed, although not found exactly in the chancel, might very probably be that of Abbot Brokehampton himself, and on inquiring what became of the remains, the clerk merely reported that 'he was chucked out,' and eventually reburied in the south of the churchyard. The skeleton was in the east wall of the transept, which was, no doubt, the chantry chapel known to have existed in the church. It is mentioned in the Chantry Certificates of Edward VI, from which I have quoted the Saintbury entry. Willersey stands thus:

Woollersey P'oche.
  Oon shepe given to ffinde a lampe there.
  The same priced att … iis.
  To the poor … nl.

The sheep, I presume, was presented annually to maintain the chantry lamp, and when the chantry was dissolved the sheep was no longer contributed, so nothing came to the poor. Whilst at Saintbury, the benefaction being in the shape of twelve pence worth rent of land, that annual amount continued and was merely diverted from the lamp to the poor.

The church itself at Willersey would no doubt be founded by Evesham Abbey, and Norman parts of it still remain. Like Saintbury it is cruciform, but larger, and differs in many other respects. At Willersey the square grey tower is central, whilst the Saintbury spire rises above the south transept. In bells they are equally rich, both having a peal of six. Those here at Willersey, probably also a recasting, are a relic of the Rudhall family, famous for several generations as bell founders at Gloucester, and they date from Queen Anne's reign. The inscriptions upon them are as follow:

1. Let me ring for Peace merrily, A.R. 1712.
2. A.R. 1712.
3. Prosperity to this Parrish. A.R. 1712.
4. Abra Rudhall Bellfounder 1712.
5. Peace & Good Neighbourhood. God save the Quun [sic].
   A.R. 1712.
6. Mr Ric. Gregory Rector Iohn Freeman William Suck Ch. Wardens 1712.

Between the initials A.R., for Abraham Rudhall, but which no doubt he thought would do for Anna Regina also, in each case is a little bell, the founder's trademark.

No, no, none of these villages seem complete without their peal of bells. These are part of the voice, I was going to say the natural voice, of this countryside. But in addition to this, the bells played also a considerable personal part in the lives of the ringers. Of course, with the rest of characteristic country life, the art of change-ringing has languished almost to extinction. I am afraid it began many years ago by a too rigorous exaction of what we are apt to call propriety in the belfry. So far as these villages are concerned, infinitely better the flagons of cider with some boisterous mirth in the belfry than that the whole society of the bells should have dwindled merely to a Sunday official function. The benefits of what was nothing less than the club of the belfry far outweighed any mere irregularity of manners. A very little real tact with individuals could have kept this within reasonable bounds, leaving at the same time a sense of freedom to the ringers. But I suppose the old habits would have died out with so much else in any case. Not only have rural tastes and recreations materially altered, but the occasions which used to call forth the voice of the bells so frequently are themselves no longer remembered or observed in parish life. I have spoken of the Restoration Day peal at Saintbury in the early morning sunlight, and I think if I had to pick out any one particular association with the bells at Willersey, I should recall the peal which ushered in St Thomas's morning (21 December) at five o'clock, as a signal that the Christmas season had begun. In the effect of this peal there was something like real enchantment, only to be likened to that solemn mystery of childhood when awakened in the dead of night by the north-country waits singing *Christians, Awake!* or *The Mistletoe Bough.* The dawning consciousness of some sweet magical sound borne upon the moaning wind, or filling the silent frost-bound air, as you turned drowsily before opening your eyes to total darkness and to a full grasp of what it all meant, cast a spell over your senses which was to last for several days. The effect of that peal alone upon the slumbering parish was greater than one can tell. Where there had been no actual consciousness of the mystical effect you could gather hints from the simplest minds that much of it had been felt, and this became all the more valuable for being so dimly recognised.

But apart from the bells, the original importance of St Thomas's Day throughout the kingdom was essentially a practical one to the poor. The custom of going the round of your parish on that day for alms in money or kind was widespread, under such names as a-gooding or a-corning. Hereabouts, of course, this is now confined to the children and is still called by them 'going a-thomasing.' There was a rhyme attending it, which I fancy is rarely, if ever, heard complete nowadays. Mr John Andrews gives me the Willersey version of it in his day as follows:

> Please to remember St Thomas's Day,
> St Thomas's Day is the shortest day,
> Up the stocking and down the shoe.
> If you an't got no apples money 'll do,
> Up the ladder and down the wall,
> A peck o' opples 'll serve us all.

It is not easy to see what the stocking and shoe had to do with it, but the ladder and wall would presumably suggest an ascent to the loft where the apples would naturally be supposed to be stored.

Whilst on this subject of rhymes I will mention here another relating to bonfire night which the same friend gave me as current in earlier years, and which as he heard it in childhood delivered by the boys outside the door left an indelible impression on his mind, evidently not without a touch of awe. At odd times during the day of 5 November, the village boys would be seen preparing heavy stakes, one of which must be in the hands of each boy who joined the group that went from door to door to beg fuel for the bonfire. It was these stakes more than the words of the chant that wrought the effect of which Mr Andrews speaks. For all the boys together beat time on the

pavement with a solemn rhythmic thud at each word as they delivered their
recitative, ending up with a hurried repetition of the last word accompanied
by a thunderous roll of all the stakes rapidly beaten on the ground together,
with a vigour which sometimes even broke the blue lias flagstones of the
farm courtyard. The words thus chanted were these:

Remember, remember, the fifth of November,
Gunpowder treason and plot
It shall never be forgot.
A stick and a stake for King Gearge's sake,
Pray, master, give us a faggit.
If you wunt give us one we'll take two,
The better for we and the wuss for you-you-you-you.

As in most of the prayer books in Saintbury Church in those days, the
name of King George, of course, remained a fixture also in this bonfire
formula so long as the rhyme was in use at all. I am told that one old
gentleman, the lawyer above referred to, certainly expostulated with the
boys and showed how the proper words 'for Victoria's sake' would fit in
just as well, but without effect. It was this same precisian who would
ask the children when a-thomasing who St Thomas was, and on their
confessing that they did not know, the old gentleman replied that he
would give them nothing till they did.

   This method of collecting wood, however, has been long disused, although
in most villages there is still some attempt at a bonfire. With thatched roofs and
rickyards around, it always surprised me that there were not serious disasters,
but I never heard of a single one caused by the village bonfires. I know
that I have looked on with some uneasiness at several great flares on Sawpit
Green with a wind carrying more than sparks right across the adjoining
Pool Farm, but such ridiculous misgivings never seemed to disturb more
reasonable mortals. Very much of the old village life must indeed have been
foregone altogether if scruples such as this had ever troubled the inhabitants.
They happily rushed into all sorts of rude and even dangerous diversions and
practical jokes with all the recklessness of children, and if calamity by any
chance resulted it was accepted as a necessary part of the scheme of things.

FOURTEEN

THE WAKE

Having now got right into the midst of the old home life of the district, it is difficult to know where to stop, but for the present, at all events, I must only select one or two prominent features to complete this bare outline of the landscape as a whole. As I have probably said often before, the whole village year was just one charming procession of homely and picturesque scenes blending with as unspoiled natural conditions as this industrial kingdom would anywhere permit. It is a pity that some visible impression of it all cannot be made permanent as a source of reflection and inspiration to all such rural parishes, in the hope of their capturing from it that sense of continuity which has been so sadly broken.

This is all hopelessly sentimental, no doubt; but then all art is sentimental, has its very roots in sentiment alone, and is it not primarily through art, pure and simple, that the civilising of an instructed rural population must lie? I know the danger of using such a word, but I shall hardly be suspected of using it in any precious or pedantic sense. I mean art at its most primitive sources. The word itself should never be heard in any village schoolroom or village institute, but the spirit of it could without much difficulty be got to pervade the whole. Cleverness is surely the last thing to be desired in country life. This, as we see, means death to the very soul of art. 'Modest doubt,' says Shakespeare, 'is called the beacon of the wise.' What country folk want is that matchless art of the nursery rhyme, old song or ballad, vernacular bird or flower name. Happily, instinctive qualities are not easily exterminated, and may lie dormant until the genial season returns which is to quicken them to life. This hope is indeed strongly supported by cultured craftsmen friends, like the late Mr Ernest Gimson for instance, who have tapped professionally the strictly rural population for the purposes of artistic handicraft work, and have found native genius in plenty ready to respond to a fostering touch. There seems no reason why other less technical imaginative qualities should not also manifest themselves in this rural life at large if awakened by a similarly enlightened sympathy.

This is a singular prelude, certainly, to my remarks on the plain old village wake as I used to know it. But I was led into the digression by that reference to the parish life as a whole in its beautiful setting, and with this the rude and boisterous mirth of the wake blends in a delightful way. Whether highly artistic in itself or not, jt was very picturesque, and the fun was so spontaneous and free from pretence as to justify any incidental roughness. It is well known that this festival is often kept on the day of the saint to whom the parish church is dedicated. It was not so at Willersey. The church is dedicated to St Peter, whose day is 9 June, and the wake is held on Midsummer Day, the 24th. This latter is the feast of St John the Baptist, and so many important popular rites were traditionally associated with this day that they may have outweighed the claims of St Peter in the eyes of the parishioners. Or, as the days were so near, possibly the feast was extended originally to include them both. I did not hear of the survival of any particularly superstitious rites in the village connected with this day. There was a regular charmer, to be sure, who died only a few years ago, but he had merely the phases of each moon to consult and could exercise his skill under the auspices of any one of them. He was said to be chiefly in request for cases of erysipelas, but seemed to be called in for any infirmity, and was firmly believed in by many. Possibly the maidens secretly practised some of the mystic divinations proper to Midsummer Eve without my hearing of them, but as a rule the later methods of learning matrimonial fortunes have little of mystery or secrecy about them.

Certainly, I shall not attempt to invest the celebration of the wake itself with any sense of magic, however full of dramatic interest it might prove if you looked closely into it. The best way to appreciate the scene from this point of view would be to give up the afternoon to wandering about the hill above Saintbury Church or the Swinging Tree, so as to get in proper tune with the summer landscape, and then as the raucous blast of Mr Curtis's hurdy-gurdy, or the first distant rumble of thunder, broke upon the sultry air, drop down to the village. The sun thickened early and the atmosphere was nearly always close and thundery that afternoon, with clouds brooding heavily over the vale. The sickly scent of elder blossom swept in waves over the roadway, drowning the later roses, but in its turn overpowered now and then by the more widely diffused smell of hay. So typical were these midsummer conditions that the old-fashioned inhabitants would tell you that the farmers used to finish hay-making on wake day, and the women of the neighbourhood looked for the regulation thunderstorm towards evening to stop their work in the fields so that they could get off to the wake. Naturally with this report was coupled blame for the farmers, who latterly have little grass cut by that day and yet grumble at being short of autumn keep. If they hained and cut the grass earlier, said the wiseacres, they would have a good lattermath.

From my own several years' experience, a thunderstorm seems indispensable to the wake, though no doubt some of the years missed it. In any case a heavy elder-scented air hangs about that blatant music which drew the first eager children to climb into their saddles. A few of the earliest corners would by then be greeting one another, or already promenading the road to be assailed by some tentative shout from a stall or Aunt Sally. From that point the proceedings rapidly developed as visitors kept pouring in. But for residents, of course, the interest had begun long before this. If you chanced to be up or awake at a late hour of the previous night when only the hooting of an owl stirred the solemn stillness of the slumbering countryside, other sounds would gradually dawn on you which on going out could soon be recognised as the rumbling of wagons and the tread of horses' feet. It was the first contingent of the vans. The sounds grew more distinct, got right up into the dark village, and with much shuffling and cries of 'Whoa!' ceased. There was a pause. All sank to a mere jingling of harness or some slight movement of a horse. Voices in quiet conversation followed, no doubt selecting a pitch, and, this decided, the silence was once more broken by the horses being put in motion. As each heavy load was hauled from the metalled roadway, its movements with a jolt sank to dull thuds upon the turf of the green, and in a short time everything had settled down and the village was silent again. Two or three cocks from their several quarters generally concluded with crowing their satisfaction at what had been going on. But even this need not be quite the end if you were sufficiently alert to stay outside or to put your head out of the window. It was after midnight, and the van folk had all turned in. Unless heavily clouded, the summer night was not really dark. The north horizon would still show its wondrous afterglow tinged with profound colour in which sunset blended with the dawn. The air was full of the scent of honeysuckle on the wall below, and so still that the strange jerky double-noted cry of Mrs Smith's guinea-fowls might come clearly all the way from Saintbury Cross, as well as the deep 'creck-creck' of the corncrake from Lampitt's Meadow in between. Small wonder that superstitions had grown up under such solemn conditions.

In the morning you generally found that there had been other arrivals later still whilst you were asleep, and all that day the stream would continue until the greens were completely possessed by a motley assembly of stalls, tents and vans, unloading their various attractions, and transforming themselves into those marvellous creations which were to draw the long-saved pence from the pockets of all ages. I do not think there was any diversion peculiar to the district. There seemed just the usual amusements of a fair. Roundabouts, swing-boats, cocoa-nut alleys and shooting galleries, with one or two monstrosities, of course, and variety of peep-shows; stalls of sweets, and brandy-snap, Birmingham jewellery and what not. No doubt Mrs Jarley, to say nothing of Mr Vincent Crummies, would have resented the idea of being associated with any such company. Nonetheless, the atmosphere was full of them both. The intimate domestic scenes you saw going on in the open air, if it was fine, beside the steps of each van, inspired a strong human interest in the individuals, and influenced your whole estimate of the later excitement of the wake itself. This was strengthened by the fact that most of the families came regularly from year to year and so became identified with the other features of the festival. The elder Mr Curtis, indeed, the original proprietor of the principal roundabout, took such a fancy to this particular spot that on relinquishing his business in favour of his son he retired with his dwelling-van to a field at Willersey, and eventually died there. From this personal atmosphere the entertainers became but another side to the native assembly that had flocked in from all the neighbouring parishes, and played as natural a part in the picture. For the rest, parted friends, relatives and sweethearts would meet here and combine interchange of gossip with the fun of the fair. My friend the old clerk of Saintbury found a special place in these associations, too, for we always celebrated his birthday on that day, though it was really the one before.

If the thunderstorm considerately held off for a few hours, or had been got over earlier, by about seven o'clock everything would be getting into full swing. The discordant organs of two, and sometimes three, roundabouts were in full blast. Men and women bawled or screamed their several attractions. The heavy swing of the boats was in the air, or the grating on the board that stopped them, cracks of the rifles, thuds of Aunt

Sally missiles against the canvas behind, tremendous blows of the beetle in trials of strength, all blended with the general uproar of voices in almost every conceivable key of raillery and laughter, from the throng which was surging to and fro in the roadway or gathered about the greens. Towards nine the first naphtha light would flare out, to be quickly followed by others, and then the peculiar smell of these primitive cressets began to add their part to the general impression of the scene. This was the signal for the younger children and strict propriety to withdraw. Not that I ever saw anything to hurt rational susceptibilities at any hour, and of course two or three policemen were in the crowd, if with no very 'severe regard of control.' But, naturally, after dark the fun became more fast and furious, youths gave fuller play to facetious humours, delighted in swinging girls to terrifying heights in the boats, squirting scent down their necks, and so on. Even in those days, however, the women seemed quite capable of holding their own and could give quite as good as they got. Personally, I preferred the thunderstorm to terminate the proceedings rather than to come as an episode earlier in the evening, with its stampede for any available shelter. There was something good in the flickering lightning and the rumble of the dark sky going on over our little comedy for an hour or two, to give a hint of the real proportion of things. Once or twice I got the impression of this to perfection, for as a rule I saw the old clerk home to Saintbury across the fields, and in descending the hill again under the gathering storm, with that fixed glow of the village at your feet spreading upwards into the unfathomable darkness which was riven now and then by a distant flash, to be followed after a time by its mysterious roll around the heavens, it was impossible to escape some imaginative detachment.

No doubt my whole recollection of the wake, too, is coloured by the unique experience of one of these especially favourable occasions. After leaving the old clerk at his door as the cottage clock inside struck eleven, I soon became aware that the long, threatened storm was already nearer than I supposed. That ominous wind was already to be heard surging in the lower elm trees, and in Ram Close came a vivid flash almost overhead with its rattling clap immediately behind it. So I lost no time in crossing the dark fields and descending the road to the village. Great dabs of water, I can not call them spots, were flung like lead on me as I reached the corner, but in a minute or two I was within my own cottage doorway amidst that powerful honeysuckle scent, when with a crash it seemed as if the whole heavens were descending in a volume of water. Two or three men were still at the shooting gallery; the organ of the last roundabout was still grinding, and the little pony within the ring pulling its weary round, when the deluge fell. Nor did this instantly stop the proceedings. Under its canvas roof the full turn was completed for those last few riders, and the pony stopped. Then through the blinding downpour came the stumbling strains of *God Save The Queen*, with which the music always loyally closed, and with them blended the full fury of the tempest. Not that there was wind after that first blast which goes in front of a thunderstorm, but I used the word tempest in the special sense of this district. Tempest is thunder and lightning alone here. A storm may be anything else without it, even to a spell merely of cold, frosty weather. Well, on that occasion those black heavens kept opening at frequent intervals, throwing the wake and the singularly green orchard trees into spectral brilliance for an instant, and then with the crash and roar of heaven's own artillery all was dark again. The battering splash of the rain, the rush of overflowing waterspouts from the eaves, continued for a long time, and it was after midnight before this perceptibly abated, though the thunder and lightning had gone over the hill to Stow, and only flitted and growled behind us intermittently.

My cottage door faced the green, so I naturally watched the storm out, wondering what had become of the itinerant population encamped there. Two or three lights were visible, and there had been no call for aid or shelter, though it was assuredly 'a naughty night to swim in.' It had all passed off evidently as a normal occurrence. So about one o'clock, when the rain had ceased, it seemed time to give it up, and I put out the lamp. On going to the open window for a last look and a sniff of that wonderful fragrance from the drenched summer herbage before closing it, I saw a lantern alight at a van nearby and heard the sound of voices outside beside it. But for this all was silent now with merely an occasional drip from the trees. I listened and could recognise women's tongues in heated conversation, catching indeed most of the very words. Knowing whose van was there and other circumstances, it was easy to grasp at once the drift of the controversy. For so it was, although carried on without a syllable of bad language, if in aggrieved and heightening tones, I knew both sides to be of unimpeachable respectability, so felt no surprise at this. The squabble was interesting as showing the speakers' regard for etiquette and wish for freedom from professional rivalry. The original complainant had evidently been the wife of the younger roundabout proprietor, who was the daughter of the elder one, to whose van she had now come to expostulate before retiring to rest after the storm. The debate was between her and her mother at first, with some snappish interposition from a younger sister, when in the usual manner the original grievance had spread to various other issues. The married daughter had no doubt come to complain of her father's trespassing on her husband's preserves by setting up his opposition roundabout. This was made clear by one of the first exclamations I had overheard and which had come from the mother. This was: 'When Albert never came to say how do you do to your father, I said, "Set up the roundabout."' This might be thought to be quibbling since they had come on to the ground at all, but that was not necessarily so, for Willersey was a convenient halting-place on the way to the next fair at Pershore in the adjoining county of Worcester, which was held two days later, and they might very well have rested there without opening out. I did not hear how this want of respect in the husband was rebutted, but amidst many words on both sides the grievance was carried by the married daughter, herself an exemplary mother of several children, to what she evidently considered as some light and improper behaviour on the part of her sister in dancing on some recent occasion elsewhere. Here the voice of the censured sister swept in, and words naturally ran higher, but these as well as the whole attitude of mind displayed were such as might have occurred in any middle-class family at that time. It was this later altercation, however, which introduced the first comic element into the situation, for the father's deeper voice now for the first time came in with the words, calmly and persistently uttered to his married daughter, who was probably by then fanning her own indignation, 'Em, Em – we only want civility.' This was the man's only part, and it sounded extremely dignified. I listened a few minutes longer, and into the clash of women's tongues continued to come from time to time, as a burden, this sedate protest, 'Em, we only want civility.'

Sometimes one or two of the visitors would stay over another day and night, but the bulk of them were packing up the next morning and during the day would set off towards Pershore to be ready for the fair on the 26th, at which the cuckoo, by the by, is said to buy a horse in preparation for his flight. The physical effect of the wake upon Willersey Green, of course, depended much upon the weather at the time, but the damage was always considerable and it took a long time for the scars to heal. The mark which remained longest was the circular groove worn by the hoofs of the pony which drew the roundabout, and this was generally prolonged by the little children rehearsing the fun it suggested by running round and round in it during the hot summer days. This reference to the children on the green recalls an incident of a very different kind I witnessed there and with which I will close the chapter. It is the only thing of the sort I ever saw anywhere, apart from its association with children. One summer morning, in those wonderful summers of the 1890s, I heard a strange sound come from the green through my open window. Unable to recognise it, I looked out and saw a really magnificent spectacle. Two gigantic shire horses were just outside on the green, standing upright on their hind feet with forelegs interlaced as if wrestling, and, whilst snorting in the weirdest possible manner, bit savagely at each other's necks. Manes and tails were streaming and eyes flashing fury. This went on for a minute or two without either seeming to gain any advantage. So they quite suddenly parted, and with a great flourish of their heels set off at full gallop across the wide green. Then came a horrible moment, for instead of taking to the road, they were bounding straight for the narrow channel of the causeway between the island cottages I have mentioned and the main side of the village street, in the very mouth of which two little children were squatting on the ground playing with something. I waited breathless to see them crushed to pieces under these tremendous hoofs, for there was not room for the horses to pass by them, when what did the noble animals do but leap clean over the children's heads one after another, and continue their wild chase past the Blue Bell into Church Lane. This is a blind lane leading only to the churchyard, through which is a footpath to the fields, closed at both ends by a little gate in the walls. I learned eventually that the chargers had cleared both these gates also and were captured in the open field beyond. As it turned out, it was a glorious sight, and as to other consequences I did not trouble to inquire what happened to the two grooms who had been sitting in the New Inn and had not only been guilty of the folly of tying up two such animals at the door near each other, but also of tying them so insecurely that they released themselves.

Once only we had a dancing bear.

FIFTEEN

ORCHARDS

Like lanes, hedgerows and other dainties of the country, real orchards will soon be a thing of the past. A fruit plantation which the commercial needs of the present day require is a very different thing. By the necessities of the case this must be scientifically ordered, with trees rigidly quincuncial and rigorously pruned, whose trunks, if they have any, are grease banded or whitewashed. They are necessary for the markets and jam factories to be sure, but they do not gather much sentiment about them. The changed conditions of life are even rapidly demolishing the old farm orchards that remained to us. The fruit money on a farm or cottage has to be taken seriously into account, so mossy old trees must be stubbed up for fuel to make room for newer, more marketable successors, and any trees worth keeping must be artificially treated so as to be brought into line with later methods and become a source of profit. Formerly the fruit was like the poultry, an unconsidered trifle, to which no self-respecting farmer would condescend to pay any account. Consequently, the orchards became one of the most charming features of the old-world farm through all the changes of the year. By being handed down from nobody knew when, and left to themselves, except for some haphazard pruning occasionally to make a few faggots, they had become as natural a part of the landscape as the common or coppice. And the birds and flowers seemed to know it. The best of them always highly approved of an old orchard.

Think of the first spring days when the pear and plum blossom is getting overworn, as old Gerarde would say, the cherry out and apple coming on, with the notes of the chiffchaff and willow wren filling the air, floating as it were on the falling petals which come glistening down into the cowslips amongst the sun-dappled grass. That must surely have been the time when Master Shallow would take no denial and was pressing Sir John to see his orchard and to eat a last year's pippin, which would then be just at mellow perfection. It made sorry appeal, no doubt, to the sophisticated knight from Eastcheap, but the touch of simple enthusiasm raises the country justice several inches in one's estimation none the less. And he had an arbour, too. Arbours and garden-houses were in great request in Elizabethan days, and according to satirists of the time they got a bad name for themselves. But most of these old manor houses of the Justice Shallows long since became the homes of tenant farmers, and supply some of the most homely and charming features of the district.

Those in daily contact with the soil, who draw their subsistence from it, blend with the other natural objects that make up the landscape. And with nothing are they more closely associated than with the orchards. From the days of childhood amongst the cowslips and the apple-blossom, under the ripening fruit, or about the old family swing which has fairly grown into the bough of some ancient Blenheim apple tree, down to the critical sampling of the cider of the last autumn of life, that precious plot enters intimately into the spirit of the farm. But from an economic point of view it is in the autumn, of course, that the heyday of orchard life is reached. Perry and cider are the staple drinks of this district, so that the orchard becomes inseparably connected with the picturesque doings of the cider mill. After reserving the trees necessary for a supply of fruit and drink for the year, the produce of the farm orchard is usually sold by auction on the trees before the August winds come to ravage them. All then stands or falls at the risk of the purchaser.

The marketable and storing fruit is more or less hand picked, but that destined for the cider mill is allowed to drop or is shaken down by a man with the lug, a long pole having a hook fastened at the point, and all this together used generally to be gathered into great heaps by white-bonneted women. But this picturesque head gear has disappeared from the villages. Still, the whole drama of the fruit gathering is yet beautiful enough, and the great mellowing piles under the orchard trees or in the long yellow wagons during those golden days of autumn contribute much to the peculiarly hallowing impression which is inseparable from harvest time. Chiffchaff and willow wren have gone like the spring blossom, and only the loud whistle of the nuthatch, or the sweet dirge of the robin, comes on the crisp falling leaves of those frosty mornings. For some weeks the whole parish is redolent of the coarser fruits in some form or other. At close quarters it is not wholly agreeable, but as wafted across the stubble and the gorgeous hedgerows over which the kestrel is hovering, it gives a characteristic flavour, so to speak, to the delicious autumn fragrance breathed by the surging south-west sweeping up from the Bristol Channel.

The actual operations of the cider mill have been amply recorded, but there is a homely charm about them which never tires. The travelling machine, either in its simplest hand form or engine driven, shares the prosaic quality of machines in general, and besides, according to old-fashioned authorities, deprives the resulting liquor of much of that peculiar character imparted by what we are apt to call the more natural process, since the apple pips are not crushed as under the old stone wheel. The real cider mill which formed as essential a part of the manor farm buildings as the barn or cow stalls is altogether picturesque. The actual structure is sometimes open from side to side and merely roofed in, but many are walled all round and enclosed with big doors like a barn. In the centre stand the circular trough and upright wheel which runs in it for crushing the fruit, and in a corner the great press. This is the only setting that can give you the full charm of the process. And few of the rustic operations embody so much of the very essence of this countryside. To see the dim interior of such a mill at work in the slanting light of a golden October or Martinmas sun is to grasp at once all the careless tranquillity of our old country life. It is no longer a harassing part of a complex problem of economics. It has fallen back into its place in the calm procession of nature, without haste or strife, and becomes just an ally of the sun in giving an added maturity, as it were, a protracted bounty, to the kindly fruits of the earth. Never mind if the product lacks some of the refinement of more elaborate manufacture. It need not really do so, if some elementary notions of cleanliness could be instilled into those whose work lies so habitually in the mire. Honest earth and water, I suppose, are harmless enough, possibly beneficial, but familiarity with this has unfortunately bred an indifference to dirt of quite another character. Indeed, scruples on the score of cleanliness are still very commonly scorned as finical by rural workers and viewed with impatient contempt. In spite of inspectors and various other expensive legislative efforts it would appal many an innocent housewife to see, for instance, the conditions under which even the greater part of the milk supplied to her children is produced at the fragrant homesteads.

But the conditions of cider production hereabouts do not concern the world at large. It is all for home consumption, and has been for many generations consumed here in quantities surprising to a stranger. Eight quarts a day was a common allowance for one man in the hay or harvest field, and I remember the old clerk telling me of a case where ten quarts were allowed. The two gallons he passed as quite a compassable potation, but the extra half-gallon he thought might present difficulties to a good many men. This necessitated vast stores of liquor on the larger farms in old days. The cellars were stocked with an array of great casks, the general size being 110 gallons, but some were made for as much as 400-500 gallons, as it was held that the strength of the cider is better preserved by a large quantity being kept together in a body. In Dr Johnson's scale of liquors I do not know where cider would have come, but from these stupendous quantities being consumed in a day it evidently does not err on the heroic side. I believe it is commonly reputed as an especially wholesome anti-arthritic beverage, but it is an odd fact that in few rural districts do you see so many disabled aged figures painfully crawling about as in these villages where the human frame has for generations been positively soaked with the juices of apple and pear. But possibly even such copious draughts of the most potent elixir would be insufficient to counteract the effects of lifelong subjection to the various forms of enervating moisture arising from a heavy clay soil.

Perhaps the strongest testimony to the unheroic properties of cider lies in the fact of its not having been celebrated in song. It was not to be expected that Master Shallow would use such mild inducement to tempt Falstaff to prolong his stay, but it is rather strange that Shakespeare has made no mention of the drink at all. If the Justice himself and cousins Silence and Slender demanded a more powerful stimulant, the serving-man Davy must have had command of cider butts for the use of himself and fellow servants in the house and on the headlands of red wheat. Without making any special search I do not remember to have met with any celebration of this beverage in local verse. Of course, the eighteenth-century *Cyder, a Poem* of John Philips is familiar enough by name to literary students at all events, and may surprise us now by its claim to be considered a poem at all, but that sprang from the county of Hereford. Whether poetry or prose, we may recall that Dr Johnson stated the eminent gardener, Philip Miller, told him 'that in Philips's *Cyder, a Poem*, all the precepts were just, and indeed better than in books written for the purpose of instructing, yet Philips had never made cyder,' and in his Life of Philips the doctor has consequently claimed that his work is 'at once a book of entertainment and science.' This further double claim on both sides of it will no doubt provoke a smile nowadays, and from Johnson himself one might rather have looked for some such disparagement of the work as we are told he extended to that other so-called poem, *The Fleece.* 'He spoke slightingly,' says Boswell, 'of Dyer's "Fleece." The subject, Sir, cannot be made poetical. How can a man write poetically of serges and druggets? Yet you will hear many people talk to you gravely of that excellent poem *The Fleece.*' One would have supposed that a sheep and its fleece in its various natural surroundings was at least as susceptible of poetical treatment as the apple and its cider. Nor less, indeed, *The Sugar Cane*, which production of Grainger's Johnson went on to ridicule as the subject of a poem. For it was the subject the doctor twitted and not its treatment. 'What could he make of a sugar canes,' cried he. 'One might as well write *The Parsley Bed, a Poem*, or *The Cabbage Garden, a Poem.*'

Whether the precepts in Philips's *Cyder* are 'better than in books written for the purpose of instructing' we need not inquire. Several good men had written before him in honest prose upon the subject, including John Evelyn, the diarist, but Philip Miller, F.R.S., 'Member of the Botanick Academy at Florence, and Gardener to the Worshipful Company of Apothecaries, at their Botanick Garden in Chelsea,' as he is proclaimed on the title page of his *Gardener's Kalendar*, at least should have been a judge of the matter. One such little book, at all events, written very distinctly for this purpose of instruction, which I happened to pick up a short time ago in a two-penny box at a bookstall, seems to me to contain both more 'entertainment and science' than the lines by the author of *The Splendid Shilling* that Johnson and Miller commended. The tract in question is dated 1707 (the year before Philips's *Cyder* was published), and it was then in its fourth edition, 'Printed and sold by J. How, at the Seven Stars in Talbot Court, in Grace-Church street.' It is written by one Sir J. More, obviously a practical enthusiast in all branches of rural economy, and who in a title page of that delightful old kind which summarises the whole contents of the book, sets forth in very distinct terms his purpose of instructing. This is just the beginning of it:

ENGLANDS INTEREST: or, The Gentleman and Farmers Friend, shewing 1. How Land may be improv'd from 20s to 8£ and so to 100£ per acre per annum, with great ease, and for an inconsiderable Charge. 2. How to make Cyder, Perry, Cherry, Currant, Goose-berry, and Mulberry Wines, as Strong and Wholesome as French or Spanish Wines:
And the Cyder and Wines so made to be sold for 3d per Quart, tho' as good as Wine now Sold for 18d.

And so on, through the raising of a nursery, orchard, brewing March or October beer, breeding horses, husbandry of bees, down to:

> 7. Instructions for the profitable Ordering of Fish Ponds and the Breeding of Fish.

And all this in a little duodecimo of 166 pages! The author's enthusiasm is boundless, not merely in respect of the pecuniary profit attending his schemes, but of the health and gaiety they would impart to the nation. 'Thus much I can honestly and truly averr from a long continued Experience,' says he. 'That a Glass of this Excellent Refined Cyder-Royal, drank half an hour before Meals, procures a good Appetite; and after Meals helps Digestion: That it cheers the Heart, and Revives the Spirits. And as for its Operation upon the Brain, when too much is drank at a time, the same is less hurtful than excess of strong Beer, Ale, Canary, or High-Country- Wines.' So possibly Falstaff was mistaken if he disposed of all cider under his 'first human principle' of forswearing thin potations and addicting ourselves to sack.

But I have wandered from the old mill, with probably a robin on the roof and the golden sun lighting up the patient revolving old white horse through the open doorway as he draws the great stone wheel round its foaming trough. Trifles, no doubt, in the practical scale of things, but if our education is to advance in any true sense, surely something of this aspect of rural affairs will at last be brought home even to the workers amongst them. How else can any taste or sentiment at all be preserved for us? We all constantly bewail the effects of our industrial and commercial system upon the population engulfed in it, yet are doing our best to reduce the solitary source of a more inspiring life to the same deadening level. With almost wholly technical instruction, and recreation almost exclusively drawn from whist drives, comic songs, jazz and fox-trot dances, or other 'latest from London' attractions which allure the rustics to our village entertainments, it is not realised that there are hardly any rustics left and that the characteristic (if unconscious) sentiments of country life are getting poisoned at the very source. It cannot be wondered at that spiked railings with a cement pavement round village crosses are tolerated; that broken bottles, pots and pans, and refuse of all sorts defile the flowery waysides and hedgerows; and that any gracious old relics of a saner life are spurned as effete and meaningless. When our country life has finally lost its memory as well as charm:

This happy breed of men, this little world,
This precious stone set in the silver sea

will be numbering its days indeed, whatever triumphant figures the statisticians may be elaborating in their blue books.

How to instil what we call taste is a very old problem, and it is very clear that the highest system of mere instruction does nothing at all to solve it. Like poesy, apparently, it is just a gift of God, but at any rate it does not seem to have been incompatible with what we are pleased to call a state of ignorance, so long as such a state was leavened by the gracious qualities of modesty, sense of restraint and of human limitations. Indeed, we know that with such a leaven ignorance itself in any unworthy sense does not exist. No gracious soul, how ever uninstructed, can ever be ignorant of what it needs to know, for it is intuitively open to every ray of illuminating influence as a natural consequence, to which the fullest load of undigested instruction is irrevocably shut. In stead of doing our utmost to assimilate the tone of country life to that of the town, one would have thought that every effort would be made in the other direction, if only for the benefit of the preponderating town itself, in order that a gracious contrasting scene and temperament might be within its reach by way of relaxation and relief from the unnatural strain of the pavement, to say nothing of any higher kind of inspiration.

Surely these orchards and meadows are to blossom again for us with a purpose beyond the mere computation of bushels and hogsheads and fluctuations of the market. It will hardly be disputed that they possess just those influences readiest to our hand for which all thinking persons are seeking in order to counteract the floundering insecurity of our emotional life. If only as a key to the treasures of our most characteristic literature and art, this imaginative outlook on our rural life and landscape is indispensable, yet those for whom this influence is most vital are drawing farther and farther away from its touch.

SIXTEEN

THE SALTWAY

There was no deliberate intention to survey the whole of Kiftsgate hundred in these pages, but as so much has been said about it in previous chapters it seems impossible to close without a glance at what on the whole is perhaps the most beautiful corner of that section of the county. After leaving Willersey, the low road I spoke of continues to wind along the foot of the hills in a south-westward direction to Winchcomb and Cheltenham. As before, every mile or two brings you to some fresh village almost more wonderful than the last, until at the old royal town of Winchcomb you are, as its name implies, landed in a veritable 'coomb in a corner,' out of which it may seem impossible to escape.

But first of all we are intercepted by a narrow arm of the county of Worcester, a mile or two wide, stretching from the vale right up on to the wolds, comprising the parish of Broadway, whose modest charm has long since penetrated even into another continent. This adjoins Willersey, and is entered at a little homestead by the roadside known as the Vineyard. The vine, still seen on some of the older houses, must long ago have been cultivated on some scale in this district, for this suggestive name lingers here and there throughout the county. Grape-wine, as it was called, used regularly to be made in a favourable season by thrifty housewives who were blessed with a vine on the side of their houses, but like cowslip and the other homemade wines this nectar must almost have vanished from the countryside. Even metheglin, that heroic old liquor which carries us to much more romantic heights, seems to have been swept away by the ravages of bee disease, but it used to be made regularly at Willersey from the washings of the honeycomb, and though getting its proper name from precise persons I have often heard it acclaimed as 'thaiglum.' One would have expected the simpler word 'mead' to have been the form in which this beverage would have been handed down by country tongues. As regards the vine, again, even if an inclement season denied a crop of grapes, we may recall Bacon's advice about planting it merely for its scent. 'Because,' says he, 'the breath of flowers is farre sweeter in the aire (where it comes and goes like the warbling of musick) than in the hand, therefore nothing is more fit for that delight than to know what be the flowers and plants that doe best perfume the aire.' In his long list of these he includes 'the Flower of the Vines. It is a little dust, like the dust of a Bent, which grows up the Cluster, in the First comming forth.' Herrick, too, we may remember, compares its sweetness to the breath of kine. Possibly, therefore, this and the beauty of its foliage mainly induced our ancestors to plant the vine against their houses rather than any material eye to its precarious crop. There is proof enough that their almost infallible taste was by no means directed wholly to utilitarian ends.

After passing through the beautiful parish of Broadway, we re-enter the county of Gloucester at Buckland. In about two miles more the wonderful village of Stanton is reached. Shakespeare himself might step into this village and feel quite at home, for it presents about the same appearance as it did in his day. Grey church spire, grey gabled mansion, grey gabled farmhouses, grey gabled cottages and grey cross in the wide open roadway at the foot of the village which straggles up the hillside under noble trees. No spot in the district presents more benignly the spirit of home and 'the constant service of the antique world.' But we must give thanks for the blessing and pass on. Even a momentary glimpse, however, of such a retrospect startles one into reflections which will not easily be thrown off. The charm which lurks behind in the natural and domestic history of the spot would demand a whole volume of its own. Amongst other things, this manor suggests thoughts of the ancient abbey of Winchcomb, to which it belonged for many centuries, and with other of these lower lands made up one of the minor hundreds of pre-Domesday times now merged in that of Kiftsgate. This bore the name of Gretestanes, and together with another adjacent hundred called Holeforde, which embraced the hill parts from Snowshill through the Guitings to Hawling, is said to have been appendant to yet another old hundred of Winchcomb. All the three are now included in Kiftsgate.

Not only was Winchcomb originally a hundred of itself, but until the time of Cnut it is even said to have been the head of Winchcombshire. All these interesting details with many more can be found at large in Mr Taylor's volume on the part of the *Domesday Book* relating to Gloucestershire, from which I have got most of my facts relating to these old hundreds. The next adjoining parish of Stanway, with its glorious barn and later lordly mansion, was at one time in the hands of Tewkesbury Abbey, and so came to be included in the Tewkesbury hundred. Beyond that secluded nook we come to the more open spaces of Didbrook and Hayles, where the hills, clothed with great woodlands until our late disastrous years, begin to make their wide curve for the corner coomb.

With our approach here to the site of two great abbeys, the landscape offers no end of new suggestions which in these closing pages I shall not now touch on. Though it hardly seemed possible, even the outlines of the landscape itself become more beautiful. You begin to lose the great vale to the north, and the hills seem determined to hem you in all round. The great unenclosed down of Cleeve Cloud, the highest point of the Cotswolds, cuts off your way to the south-west, and from the head lands and outliers thrown from the main range far into the vale – Langley, Dixton, Oxenton, Bredon, and Dunibleton Hills – you feel surrounded by hills, whilst through the gap between Oxenton and Bredon you get a peep of the distant blue Malverns from a different angle. At Hayles, though, in addition to an exquisite situation and the ruins of the Cistercian abbey, we may strike an old roadway which is full of interest and to which I must devote a few words. I have confessed a weakness for an ancient track, and this one now referred to is nothing less than the old Saltway by which that precious product was conveyed from Wiche (identified as our present Droitwich) to Lechiade for shipment on the Thames. It is scarcely necessary to speak of the vast importance of salt in the diet of medieval days, and no doubt a good deal of the epidemic scourges afflicting the population then might be traceable to an insufficient supply on one hand and excess on another. Salt fish through Lent, and salted meat through the greater part of the year, would alone make great demands, and on this account many of these Gloucestershire manors are recorded in *Domesday* as having one or more *salinae*, salt springs or pits, in Worcestershire appurtenant to them. Thus 'Stanwege i sauna apud Wicham.' This represents Stanway, of course, which as already stated belonged to the great abbey of Tewkesbury, and no doubt all the abbeys would take care that the various manors they were possessed of should carry sufficient salinae apuci Wicham to supply the great demands of their establishments.

This old Saltway is traceable over the hills to Hayles, and from thence passed by Toddington to the still named Saltway Barn at Hinton-on-the-Green, where it leaves the county of Gloucester on its way through that of Worcester to Droitwich. *Domesday* records that the owner of Toddington held at Wich one hide and had there seven salt pits, which rendered fifty mittas of salt. 'Although the salt was not produced in our shire,' remarks Mr Taylor in his work already referred to, 'it is by no means improbable that it was further refined on its arrival there. The most costly item in the manufacture is fuel for evaporation ... It is remarkable that the neighbourhood of Toddington and of Thornbury, where most salinae are mentioned in Gloucestershire, were both districts where much wood was to be found, and where in consequence the process of refining could be completed more cheaply than near the brine springs where the demand for fuel was so great. Apart from the manufacture of the salt it is stated that a portion of the profits of the manor of Chedworth (over the hill towards Cirencester) were derived from the toll of the salt which came to the hail; the Saltway passes very near to Chedworth.'

Although a parish with a little church of its own there is no sort of a village at Hayles. It consists just of a farmhouse or two with their buildings, the church, and the remains of the abbey, scattered delightfully about the open meadows at a distance from one another. To add to its charm there is no real road leading to the spot. A cartway with a hedge on one side and open on the other turns into a field from the highway, and this, intersected by gates as you pass from one field to the next, brings you to a park-like seclusion at the foot of the hills to ascend which the open sandy-coloured track forks in two directions over the great green field where the cows are grazing. One way past the church and abbey ruins skirts Hayles Wood on the slope up to Farmcote and Stow; the other by a farm orchard is our old Saltway, which soon becomes merely a rugged track for farm purposes, traversing the irregular pastures in its ascent of the wolds. The first summit still bears the name of Salters' Hill, which is just over 800ft. Here the road coming up Sudeley Hill from Winchcomb is reached, and from that point the Saltway enters the real grey stone-wall hill country. But in pursuing its solitary way over these silent downs, by the barley lands, the green pastures and thorn brakes, and the dreamlike grey villages, it will find no fairer view than this from the top of Sudeley and Salters' Hill. The great 'corner coomb' and the green 'south glade' amidst the woodland, that led our Saxon forefathers to attach their names of Winchcomb and Sudeley to the places before us, lie there nestling at our feet. The hills I have mentioned close in the prospect a few miles off, and away to the north-east alone is there the glimpse of a far horizon which you can hardly help fancying is bounded by the sea. Though so rich and finely wooded there is a bold irregularity about the abrupt slopes and the grouping of the hills, backed by the great open down of Cleeve Cloud, which forbids any suggestion of merely soft luxuriance. There is a stimulating hint of wild open spaces, too, and of bracing winds. At a height of 900 or 1,000ft even in a rich country you can get a touch of that tonic exhilaration which is the peculiar property of the hills. Indeed, some of us may feel that full appreciation of the lower-lying beauty and luxuriance can only be fully gained by its association with these bare neighbouring heights. They have, of course, nothing in common with the stern spirit of the moors, but there is the wild freedom inseparable from extensive commons with their fragrant gorse bloom, their linnets and stonechats, and sweet plaint of the lapwing. In the fine turf of Cleeve Cloud, too, bespangled as it is with yellow tormentil and rock rose, you may even find in places sprigs of real heather, which manages to blossom in its time, and brings an interesting hint of a far distant period when a very different soil and vegetation clothed these hills.

But I must not wander away in that direction now. I merely ascended the hills again to see the old Saltway off, so to speak. This upper part which it now threads on its way to the Thames was, for a few miles more, part of the old hundred of Holeforde, which, with Gretestanes, has long been merged in Kiftsgate. I have no idea from what these two old divisions get their names, but I should like to know. To any who dabble in our landscape story at all, the very names of places afford no small part of the attraction, and perhaps none hold greater interest than those given to the different hundreds. It is not only that they carry you back so far. In addition, wherever you go through the counties, so many of these have a peculiarly picturesque suggestion about them, in spite of the etymologists forbidding us to see in them more than a purely matter-of-fact application. Even if this has to be granted, there seems some higher play of imagination about such names as Kiftsgate, Tibbald Stone and Grumbold's Ash, than East Seventeenth Street for instance. What's in a name? The worst of it is we seem to lose so much else besides with this decay of imagination. The outcry which has so frequently to be raised by the few in the effort to save some pre-eminent scene or object of beauty from destruction might be heard regularly in every parish in the land if any consistent attempt were to be made to stay the hand of reckless and needless destruction which is stretched so remorselessly over the landscape.

Nor is it this fanciful beauty or historic value alone that is at stake. It is hardly realised to what an extent byways and footpaths, for instance, not much used, in remote parts of the country are being filched from the public by being made impassable or quietly hedged in altogether. There is, it is true, an excellent Commons and Footpaths Preservation Society, but it is impossible to invoke the aid of such a central body in every petty case of this infringement of public rights. In many districts the local authorities, who should be the natural guardians of such rights, are singularly remiss in prompt and energetic action, and it is naturally invidious for a local private individual to take up the fight against such encroachments. Whatever complaints may have been just in former days against the old landed proprietors, it is certainly long since any of these offended in this respect. On the other hand, one may safely say that it is just their rights and even common liberties that have been shamelessly violated for many a day, and it is clearly they who are still regarded as the only legitimate victims of spoliation. In nearly all cases it is the newcomers without any familiar associations with their possessions who hasten to intermeddle with ancient usages. The importance of this apparently small matter need hardly be insisted upon, for it is obvious to all that, since every available road throughout the kingdom is being robbed not merely of its safety and quiet but of its secluded leisurely curves and its untrimmed natural beauties, every rugged byway and footpath over the fields and coppices become more and more indispensable to the public, as much for foot traffic as for imaginative delight. Richard Jefferies long ago advised us always to get over a stile by the roadside when wandering in the country, and such a recommendation can be very much more than confirmed in these later days. Over the grass and behind the hedges lies now our only hope of any spark of intimacy with the things we come into the country to seek. It becomes, therefore, merely an obvious duty of every district and parish council to guard jealously every one of their rights of way. Not only should the clerks of every one of them have very visibly marked on the 6in ordnance map of their several districts all the footpaths still existing, as well as any disused ones that may be recoverable, for the purposes of public inspection, but such a marked map should also prominently hang in every village club and every village school. Indeed, why should not the latter hang such a map on their wall, with not only these old footpaths clearly marked but also the names of all the fields and any object of beauty or historical interest plainly indicated? All the elder children could be instructed in the meaning of it, and as a matter of course should on leaving be familiar with all its details. Anything that presents the familiar surroundings to a rural mind from the outside, so to speak, in other than a purely practical and workaday manner from the very beginning, takes it a very great step in the right direction.

Talking of maps, I shall never forget the effect of one on an elderly miller in the south part of this county whom I met with several years ago whilst trespassing over his fields where was no pretence at a footpath. He stood to await my coming up to him, and as he did not seem to suspect me of poaching or breaking his fences, his gaze was simply one of stolid curiosity. We passed the day to each other, and I told him where I had come from and for what point I was making. I hadn't come the best way, he said. With a smile I told him I thought I had, and passed a compliment on his beautiful situation and landscape. But I must have lost my way, since I admitted I was a stranger and had never been in the neighbourhood before. No, I never lost my way. The village I wanted was not more than a mile over there, I pointed out to him, and I should soon reach the lane beyond his old mill, which, by the by, was not even visible from where we stood. Then to avoid mere suspicion and distrust I produced my map and explained the matter to him. But even then he was puzzled and not quite satisfied. This, I could see, arose from sheer amazement and not from any doubt of me. He gazed at the map in bewilderment. I strongly suspected that he couldn't read, though I did not ask a confession of the fact. He did say, however, that he had had no schooling, and positively he had never heard of such a thing as a map. It all became pure magic to him, and after some further talk and explanation the man took a childlike delight in testing me in the names of farms and villages round about us. It beat all he had ever heard of. But no, unfortunately, I could not tell him the names of his fields, so in exchange I got him to tell me them, and many other delightful old things as well, in the course of half an hour's stroll around his home before we parted.

SEVENTEEN

WINCHCOMB

It would perhaps have been better to rest content with that glimpse from the Saltway of old Winchcomb nestling in its hollow, since the closing pages of a book like this afford no space for touching even the fringes of the natural and historic interest of this spot and its adjacent manor of Sudeley. As these two places, however, which together occupy this secluded valley, afford both in scenery and story a wealth of romantic charm outstripping any of the other spots I have mentioned, and as they have been so frequently referred to, I must give them a parting glance. Not that the present Winchcomb can in any way approach the architectural beauty of Chipping Campden, but in every other aspect it goes far beyond the lovely old wool town. It is not to commerce that Winchcomb owes its rise and interest, for, over 1,200 years ago, it was a residence of the Mercian kings, and goes back to such names Offa, Kenuif, and the boy-King Kenelm of tragic legend. King Offa built a nunnery here which was replaced by a mitred abbey of the Benedictines some years later by his son King Kenulf, founded in 797. The great Archbishop Wilfrid of York dedicated it, attended by thirteen bishops, and to celebrate the solemn occasion the Mercian king set free before the altar his captive Eadbert, King of Kent. This was nearly 500 years even before the foundation of the Cistercian settlement at Hayles, such a period, let us remember, as would bring us from the reign of King John to the time of Dr Johnson.

But, needless to say, every vestige of royal residence, and even of the great abbey itself, has long since disappeared.

With such an origin there is nothing surprising in the fact that the settlement became the centre of a Winchcombshire. Although all this Cotswold district, after its abandonment by the Romans, was first taken from the Welsh, or Britons as we generally call them, and colonised by a tribe of West Saxons from the south and south-west known as Hwiccas it soon fell into the hands of that middle kingdom of Mercia which was established by the valiant old heathen Penda, advancing from the north-east. It was at any rate subdued and regarded as part of the kingdom of Mercia, whilst at first allowed to retain its own leader or under-king. When at length it came within the fold of Christianity this Hwiccan kingdom, consisting of our present counties of Gloucester, Worcester, and part of Warwick, was raised into a bishopric with its see, not at Gloucester, but at Worcester. This city, therefore, would seem to have been regarded as the capital of the Hwiccan country, and its very name is held by some authorities to have worn down from Hwic-wara-ceaster, through Wigraceaster, to our present form of Worcester. One cannot escape these thoughts in contemplating what we may call the graves of old Winchcomb. Not only do these links of history people the landscape with a whole pageant of wondrous ghosts, but they surely impart, too, a singular solemnity to the very flowers that grow here under our feet as we think of them having grown also under the tread of that long succession of picturesque forerunners. I do not care to feel how many years ago it is since, among my early visits to Winchcomb, I came tramping along the hills to Spoonley Wood to seek the remains of the Roman villa when first discovered there, but I have never quite lost the impression left by those quiet Sudeley fields that far-off summer day. Of the Roman remains in the district I have said nothing at all, but like all the rest of the invaders these great colonists soon found out the attractions of this fertile region, and have no doubt left traces of themselves in many of our household vegetables and methods of husbandry as well as in merely structural relics and place names. The Spoonley villa itself is nothing compared to those at Chedworth and elsewhere, but the walk to it at the head of that green coomb through the Sudeley meadows from Winchcomb affords about all that a bit of purely typical English landscape can supply in the way of restful charm. I have already said that the main deficiency hereabouts lies in the streams. You come to nothing that a north-country man would call 'a water.' The little river Isbourne, formed here by two or three streams gathering together from these hills, is merely a muddy brook as it runs through the beautiful hollow below the bank along which the town of Winchcomb stretches. None of the 'toddling din,' the ceaseless talk and sparkling laughter of the tiniest beck or burn of the mountains. But how ungracious such a thought becomes in the face of all this beauty. Worse than that, it is simply stupid. I hate comparisons, and in landscape especially seek to enjoy the characteristic beauty which happily even yet no individual parish in the land is totally without. What we call nature is pretty sure to act in the best of taste. It is only our perverted aims which bring in the spoiler's hand. And under this, as elsewhere, even the poor little Isbourne has too obviously suffered, It is not merely honest clay that sullies her current. In many parts both bed and bank are defiled in a way very far from nature's intentions. Fringes of sedge, loose-strife, and water mint under the withies can render even a clay bottom fragrant and beautiful, especially if the flashing kingfisher and dragon-fly were permitted to frequent their native haunt.

Parallel to this brook, and raised a little on the bank above it, runs the central town of Winchcomb in one long street. As this is the north bank, the houses occupying the south side of the street have gardens behind them sloping down to the edge of the stream, of which nothing could be suspected from the pavement. To see the beauty of this situation you must get into the houses, or go to the meadows below. The street itself is mostly narrow and does not really do justice to the old town, though, of course, as is inevitable in this district, there are several individual houses possessing all their ancient charm. Many no doubt will be built almost entirely of the abbey stones, but in any case they have all grown out of the hills around, and therefore have mellowed to that exquisite grey tint of which I have already so frequently spoken.

Of all the social and domestic lore which they enshrine I shall say nothing. To avoid temptation I will return to the heights, not this time by way of Sudeley but by the Lang-ley rising on the north-west of the town. This 'long meadow,' glade or whatever we like to call an open stretch of grass land in what would be a thickly wooded country at the time the name was applied, spreads up the slope to Langley Hill, though now divided into more than one field. A cart track of the right colour ascends it, past a little farm near the top, to the quarry which crowns the summit at a height of 900ft. Though we complain of the loss of trees it is wonderful how well wooded any really rural district of England still seems to be. Much has gone from these parts, but there is abundance of noble trees to glorify the landscape yet, fortunately just here with hardly any of the ubiquitous larch or fir in sight. There must have been vast stretches of natural woodland formerly, for in the *Domesday Book* the manor of Sudeley is credited with 8,000 acres wood, an area about four times the size of the whole parish now. I suppose there is no means of knowing in what direction all this lay. This *lang ley*, at any rate, would be green and open, facing almost due south, and giving, as it does today in ascending the slope, perhaps the finest glimpse to be had of this secluded corner coomb. The woodpeckers laughed, the jays cursed and the magpies chuckled to those old warriors and husbandmen as they do to us. The flowers in the grass would be much the same, and no doubt the track up to the quarry goes back to as early a time. As on all these hills, there was of course a camp up here, and indeed many of the other allurements of the skyline which most of us love and which drive us occasionally to exclaim with Shelley:

> Away, away from men and towns,
> To the wild wood and the downs,
> To the silent wilderness,
> Where the soul need not repress
> Its music, lest it should not find
> An echo in another's mind,
> While the touch of nature's art
> Harmonizes heart to heart.

This becomes really the only way now of getting what you seek from the country, for the general rush begins to defeat its own ends and the poor country is rapidly expiring under our boisterous caresses.

Yet, if honestly admitted, there is at times a longing in every soul for a real cloud, a free bird and a wild flower. Every child is born with it, and none become too old to know that one sunny hour spent with any or all of the three carries a mysterious benediction such as no other relaxation can bestow. And there is the wind on the heath, too. Not one of us ever quite loses the gipsy that is in us. If you doubt it go and startle the kestrel from the quarry, and lie in one of the old over grown hollows by the thistles to watch the bird wheel and then hover with quivering or even motionless wings flashing brown and white against the breezy blue sky. Happily it is still a sight which may be familiar enough to any eyes in this district, and there are few which can give a more joyous sense of freedom. It is none the worse if it should very likely end in one of nature's squabbles, for, though comparatively harmless, the kestrel by all birds is counted a hawk. Everybody seems to buffet him, but particularly a crow or rook. The odd part is I never chanced to see a kestrel either attack or retaliate. Even a pair of nesting lapwings will hustle him off their ground. So far as my slight observation goes, crows and rooks wage the most inveterate warfare of all against him. One of them will keep up the contest until your eyes or glasses can follow it no longer. But it is a bullying chase rather than a contest. Quite secure in his agility, the kestrel silently flies on, swoops and dodges, whilst the angry crow tumbles about him with vicious but futile digs of the beak and incessant petulant croaks. I should think the magpie on the whole works far more mischief to his fellow birds than the kestrel, yet you don't often see him assaulted. Perhaps the villain is only known as an enemy by the smaller defenceless birds.

The last kestrel I saw was yesterday, and he was driven off by mere clatter. Whilst passing over a field bordered by some tall elms, the silence was suddenly broken by the shrill outcry of two of our recently established little owls. During the last few years they have become increasingly abundant in this district, and though there is a touch of a wild scream about their cry, I am obliged to call it a squeal or yelp, for there is a rather too sharp abruptness in it, and, so to speak, a little jerk or joint, which reminds you of a fractious little terrier. Well, two of them set up this cry quite suddenly together, as even three or four of them often will, and on looking in that direction I saw a hen kestrel come flying from the trees. But she flew off alone, followed by nobody, and the cry immediately ceased. So I concluded the outcry of the little owls and the swift flight of the kestrel had some sort of connection. The kestrel soon hovered over the field for a short time, but catching sight of me flew quite away. The owls kept to their trees, and in spite of all my efforts I failed to get even a glimpse of them. To me they seem an extremely difficult bird to observe and I have only caught sight of a very few, though their cry is heard perpetually through the fields. Their dusky colour is strongly in their favour, and though standing under a tree in which one has cried or is still crying, I fail to detect him with good field glasses. Even throwing stones into a tree will not as a rule move him. I am ashamed to say that as the bird is not in our British Bird books I have not yet looked up the recorded particulars of its life. Since it is now getting so widespread, it is hardly necessary to state that it is habitually a day owl, but as I have never seen it feeding I am ignorant of what it feeds on. From its first appearance (about five years ago) it has never aroused any open hostility in other birds here, so far as I have seen or heard. It was accepted as a day bird from the outset, and so spared the fate of other owls. Let a poor brown or barn owl drift out into the day, and the whole nation of birds will chivy him from tree to tree in a crowd with a veritable babel of scolding.

The squeal or yelp of this newcomer of course just suited the starlings, and many of them have added it in perfection to their various accomplishments. But I have never heard one of them attempt another note of the little owl which is of a much more suggestive nature, and which in my present ignorance I like to attribute to the hen bird. It was indeed this impressive note which first puzzled the ear of this neighbourhood and drew attention to the newcomer. It should really be called a double note, and is of a wonderfully mournful and solemn tone, uttered slowly and at brief intervals for an hour or two together. The only thing I can liken it to, and which it very nearly resembles, is that wary anxious note of a curlew hidden in the heather, with head just raised above it, on becoming aware of a human approach before flying up. 'Whaa-up – whaa-up'. The first syllable deep and drawn out, the last slightly raised and briefer. It seems a singular fact to me that since the complete establishment of the bird in these parts this attractive voice has virtually ceased. It has got less and less frequent year by year, until this year I have only once heard it and that was in the early spring. The blatant yelp alone now seems to satisfy the whole of the little owl nature. Ornithologists may have some quite simple explanation of this grievous loss, but in my romantic fancy I like to put down the frequency of those sad notes during the first year or two to the supposition that they came from the disconsolate pioneer hens who had travelled here first and did not succeed for some time in inducing mates to follow them.

All this is not quite such a digression as it seems, for one of the few little owls I have chanced to see was startled by my approach to the quarry on Langley Hill. I saw it through my field glasses not far off, but unfortunately not until it had risen from the lower stones and was flying over the rim above, so there was no chance of learning what it had been at. A kestrel and a magpie also habitually haunt that spot. But as I said at Saintbury and Willersey, what of the real or imaginary does not haunt a Cotswold quarry? They are amongst the most seductive spots of the landscape. Quite apart from the active life about them, the mere light and colour with which the very stones are infused add a peculiarly characteristic smile to the features of the brown old earth. This did much, no doubt, in inspiring our forefathers with their faultless taste. Being so much nearer to the heart of primitive nature themselves, they merely carried on its processes a step farther by a touch of human art in the homes they built, in the little garths, orchards, and roadways they constructed. We may smile at the simplicity of it all, but it is as well to remember the store of reserve strength that lies in simplicity and restraint, to say nothing of all the wealth of character which has sprung from reverence and love of home.

EIGHTEEN

SCENERY AND STORY

A s I set out merely with the intention of trying to give in words some slight impression of this particular bit of English landscape, with glimpses of the past life upon it, I am afraid I have moralised the spectacle far too much already. But in view of the fate which seems to hang over our cherished land it seems impossible to escape this vein of reflection. And in resolving to make this my last chapter I will shamelessly plunge into a few more concluding, sentiments on what appears the vital spirit of the scenes I have been recalling. So in order to end as and where I began, I went off yesterday to the top of Saintbury Hill.

In the cold but sunny east wind which has come at last to dry up the water-logged land, so that we may at least begin to think of preparing for our first spring seeds, I looked at the old scene once more and felt how idle it was to attempt in this way to present its material features, much less to put into words the faintest expression of what it all means to us. The grey film which had over spread the sky from early morning was breaking up and turning itself into uncarved smoky clouds, with great seas of blue amongst the fringes, from which the sun at first threw merely patches of hazy light over the wide landscape towards Bredon. Such a wind allows little colour, but gives some compensation in this softening haze which throws such beautiful mystery over the details of the land. There were not even the purple heads of the blossoming elm trees near by, for during the past extraordinary season (1922-3), winter we can hardly call it, these were best at the end of January, and the cold rain of February battered them too soon to a dull lifeless brown. Yet now spring was in the air and at my feet, and here was all the old alluring charm, bringing with it the inevitable sense of loss and waste of this boundless material, confessedly enchanting to the whole civilised world, and through which so many of our best national characteristics have been built up. Happily, unconsciously built up, of course. But unfortunately the childhood of our world has passed, and with it very much of the childhood even of our simple rural life. It is no longer possible to live merely by heaven-born instinct, so we are trying to put something deliberate in its place. In the country quite as much as in the town, life now requires an art, as even Wordsworth, the poet of Nature and simplicity, at last admitted. But in the country our motive may be said to be almost directly opposite to that which actuates the town. It is not to hide, and forget our intolerable surroundings that we need culture and recreation in the country. We need it to open our eyes to the things that are about us, to make us see them more clearly and so be able to enjoy them more completely.

Praise of the past and complaints of the present are no new themes in country or any other life, and we all in turn claim that the world jogs on very well in spite of all the querulous laments of each penultimate generation over the general tendency of things. Still, I suppose we all agree that there have always been periodically in the world's history waves of national disintegration which destroy not only certain elements of social life, but also material features of beauty and interest, which seem never to be restored, and the loss of which succeeding generations continue to deplore. It can scarcely be denied .that the country life and landscape of England is now assailed by such a wave, and one, moreover, of ominous and unprecedented breadth and volume. Of course it had been gradually gathering during the life of the oldest of us, but it looks now very much like the curling of the crest. I leave the economic side of the question for the present wholly out of my view, for that can always look after itself. It is the spiritual, imaginative, sentimental (call it what we will) side of it that ought to give most concern to us, for it is obvious the most scientifically administered instruction does no more in this direction than economics or mere amusement. For the really country-minded folk that matter there seems little doubt that enlightened sentiment alone can go to those simple imaginative sources which we want to touch again. Any amount of pure and simple amusement will never do this. It seems the blindest absurdity for highest culture to find so much of its best inspiration in the idealised life and landscape of the country without taking the most earnest steps to direct that life and landscape itself into the light which the great idealists have shed around it. Our present course of instruction with the boundless dissemination of more or less urban amusements go positively against this by extinguishing altogether the peculiarly rural characteristics we are so anxious to preserve and exalt.

Though we are not as a race thought to be a literary or artistic people, nevertheless I suppose it is admitted that some of the most exquisite products of human genius in literature and the arts have been directly inspired by our British landscape. Yet in what way does this influence our village life? Do not let us forget with what emotion many of our soldiers in those ghastly trenches, and our sailors on the death-sown sea, read poems and songs and romances which breathed the spirit of their homeland, but which they had never thought of reading or of feeling until torn away from it. They found rest and inspiration from those few moments in that placid atmosphere which only art can give. It seems sometimes to be imagined that a learned education is necessary to understand literature and art. But country folk need not trouble their heads in the least about that. That is not the art they require. If they are content to enjoy what others understand they will have no difficulty, but above all let them be sure they do enjoy and make no pretences. Happily most of the very highest in literature and art is the simplest to understand and appeals to every one of us. Indeed, all who feel a moment's joy in a country walk, all children who love and cull a country flower have surely got the right perception of the very source of all art.

Sad platitudes no doubt all this, on the very elements of current education. But I am content to have it so since I gather my impressions only from the actual countryside, and as they will scarcely be contested by those in contact with it from day to day, no harm can be done by dinging in our ears first principles so imperceptible in their results. Their application is possibly not simple or not sincere enough to take effect. There can be little doubt that we get farther and farther away from the real root of the matter, if our object honestly is to create a rural population whose joy and contentment in their surroundings are to put their social and economic conditions alike on a sound and prosperous footing. If we leave the tangled problem of religion wholly out of the question, there can be no more promising material for the leavening of country minds than this of the objects around them in all their inexhaustible aspects. In this, as in nothing else, all can unite. It may appear pedantic and tiresome to keep harping on that catchword 'Shakespeare's country,' but if this could ever be made more than a hollow lip-word, could ever be brought home to our nation as really significant of a matchless spiritual ideal to which that inscrutable soul allures us, then the reiteration of his name and country could never be pressed too persistently on our ear. It is impossible to have known this district intimately for about half a century without an infinite sense of gratitude for the part it has played in giving one the best of commentaries on Shakespeare. The poet's own landscape and his works, of course, inevitably act and react upon each other. Neither could be quite the same without the other. So many of the flowers your eye lights upon, of the words and phrases you hear let fall, of the homeliest incidents of wood and meadow all around you, are virtually those that he saw and drew upon, so are enshrined in the halo which his genius has cast about them, and to see all these actually around you today deepens the spell which that genius in its turn has cast.

Brooding like this inevitably brought up once more the figure of my dear old Adam, the clerk, sexton, and road-mender of Saintbury, who embodied it all, and who was 'not for the fashion of these times.' The mere thought of him seems to present an epitome of the whole story and scenery of this countryside. For not only was he himself so natural and picturesque a feature of the lax but he was, so to speak, its memory also for at least 150 years, if we couple with his own experiences those handed on to him by the grand fathers of his youth. The vast span of his reminiscences, covering just those homely details of rural life which are lost like last year's flowers, all so naturally, casually and vividly related in a speech matchless for the purpose, made a combination which could not but impress you with all the effect of a bit of nature's art. Nor can I part with him here without recalling the deep tones in which he used to give that gracious old toast of his on various occasions in the words 'wishing you health, ma'am, here and hereafter,' nor omit from this slight record of him the typical ending of one of his latest letters now before me, in similar words. It was written when he was close upon ninety:

Wishing you all the happiness this temporal state
affords and eternal happiness hereafter,
I am your sincere Friend
WM. SMITH
The old Clerk.
P.S. Excuse errors.

Not that there were any errors to excuse. The old hand had shaken once or twice in handling the pen over a letter of four sides, but it remains a touching and even remarkable memento of a hand which was hard with the outdoor manual labour of eighty years.

Naturally, I say, all this came back to me vividly as I stood on that ancient moot bill near to which I first set eyes on this venerable figure. I liked to fancy him as typifying our best aim in country life itself. Though wholly unconscious of his surroundings, he himself was an illustration of them all, both of picture and memory, in their simplest and most irresistible form. And these are the foundation of any enlightened content in the homely routine of rural life, therefore of all efficiency and prosperity in it as a whole. Of course, if we are content to abandon such life altogether, and by taking 'the long view' turn it merely into a department of industrial, enterprise worked by electricity from urban centres, there is an end of the matter, but I do not think the solid body of public opinion really meditates such a course, although it may be unconsciously allowing things to drift towards it. There is still a wide love of our priceless heritage as well as appreciation of its value, if coupled with a singular ignorance of the gravest symptoms of its decay. As I have admitted, all my old friend's artistic sense was exhausted on music. Scenery, bird or flower stirred no sort of emotion in him so far as I could see. But to any bit of history or imaginative lore that you could associate with any of the three he was immediately awake. There is nothing surprising in this. An aesthetic sense is rare in any class, and is obviously becoming very much rarer. But all love a story, and in country folk especially no gossip goes so readily as that upon incidents and characters of the past associated with the spots familiar to them. It seems odd that more was not made of this instinct from the very outset of our rural popular education. Richard Jefferies not only knew, but was, a countryman, and he always contended that the material most appealing to peasants was the historical. Nevertheless, could we find any rural parish in the land where any one of the strictly rural inhabitants could give the simplest intelligent account of the growth of his parish as a whole, or the historical associations of any single feature within it? If he or she could ever do that it would not be long before some sense of beauty would follow, and with these perceptions on the way the lost ideas of home might even be recaptured and rural discontent in any case rapidly decline.

As the sun is disappearing, a red ball behind the orchard trees, the pious blackbird is soliloquising all sorts of solemn moralities outside my window. I have only just become aware of it, but these notes must unconsciously have been giving me the tune, for it is hardly possible to escape solemnity when his song is filling the silent air and subtly pervading all your senses without being definitely associated with the ear. Even when the air is full of 'the charm of birds,' as the confused medley of many voices is called here, the blackbird's note always seems to form the reflective undertone of the whole, and gives what the old ballads might call 'the o'erword of the song.'Yet, although so solemn, it is full of cheerfulness, contentment and hope, those homely old virtues we like to associate with country life, and without which certainly no country life can ever be considered as existent at all. Besides, goldfinches are increasing wonderfully these years, and begin to flash around us on all hands with their sweet twitter and inimitably tender call, so clearly we are not yet at the end of all things. Indeed, yesterday on Saintbury Hill, amongst the rest, something reminded me vividly of the inspiring conditions under which at midnight I welcomed in this new year of 1923, and, with the thought, the landscape could hold nothing but its old potent charm. It was not at that spot, but several miles farther along the hills. Save by the calendar it could not be called winter, for there had been none. Flowers had bloomed abnormally from autumn on till then, and the new shoots on the garden roses were already several inches long. The old year was dying in spring-like cloud and rain until the middle of his last day. Then the sullen sky, which had even blended with the hills at first, began to lift and take some shape, so that it could be seen to move from the north with just the slightest inclination to the west. There is some magic in that wind which was not to fail us. The stormcock whistled loudly in the morning, as both he and the song thrush had done pretty regularly since October, but it was a cheerless day, though the sky continued clearing. It was from twilight, during those very last hours of the old year, that the real beauty of the scene began. The moon had got high by then, being only three days from the full, and was clear as could be, except when hidden and beautified by a passing cloudlet. These were of that faultless kind which we nearly always get here from any point of the north-west by day or night. These passed, however, and for a time the sky seemed perfectly cloudless. But when I next went out, summoned by the sound of distant bells proclaiming the approach of midnight, everything was more beautiful than ever. My nearest peal chanced to be a little more than a mile away, so there was no disturbance from any bells too near at hand. The numerous peals travelling more or less distinctly from varying distances came with impressive effect over the mysterious moonlit landscape for many miles around.

Round both the shires they ring them
In steeples far and near.

I was out of the range of Saintbury and Willersey, but could hear six or seven others in the marvellous serenity of that night. Behind all the lesser peals came booming right across the great vale the deep tones of Evesham Abbey, and I felt pretty sure that once or twice at least I caught the voice of western Tewkesbury also. There was no ringing out to the wild sky. Just the slightest touch of frost was in the air, but not a breath of wind. Exquisite patches of snow-white clouds were overhead, with profound blue rifts in them as of ice, and as they passed silently before the clear moon they produced that most beautiful of night effects, a circle of blue and orange light around the orb, veined with the markings of the cloud. These travelled comparatively quickly, though we were in absolute stillness below. A few minutes before the clock struck, the bells sank to a solemn toll, and the old year was gone. Then for New Year's morning they suddenly broke again into jubilant peals. Two or three owls were hooting off and on all the time, and just after midnight came the plaintive notes of a plover from a distant field, aroused, I suppose, by the bells. Amidst such a scene, and to such a unanimity of voices, how escape thoughts of the heart of England?

THE END

Other titles published by The History Press

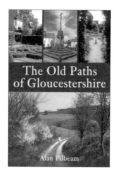

The Old Paths of Gloucestershire

ALAN PILBEAM

A walk around the old paths of Gloucestershire is, in many ways, a walk through the history of Gloucestershire itself. In this fascinating account, Alan Pilbeam tours the county's pathways and roads, demonstrating how the evolution of Gloucestershire society over time is reflected in changes in both the uses and nature of the county's footpaths. Including 100 high-quality photographs, it is also an excellent introduction to walking in Gloucestershire and will prove invaluable to both visitors to the area and locals wanting to know more about the place in which they live.

978 0 7524 4540 3

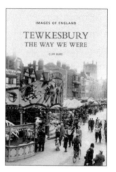

Tewkesbury: The Way We Were

CLIFF BURD

The county town of Tewkesbury stands on a flood plain, surrounded by water on all sides, with two major rivers and several smaller brooks which have always flooded. Flooding in the nineteenth century through to 2007 and Tewkesbury's most severe flood in living memory, will bring back graphic memories of how the people of the town worked together to overcome these difficult times. This volume endeavours to show how leisure activities have changed over the past century with many of the images showing sporting groups, fairs and festive activities.

978 0 7524 4692 9

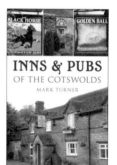

Inns & Pubs of the Cotswolds

MARK TURNER

The Cotswolds are home to some of England's finest and much-loved historical inns and pubs. This A-Z covering Gloucestershire, Oxfordshire, Warwickshire and Worcestershire is a delightful tour around the most interesting pubs in the area. Taking in all manner of establishments such as the Coach & Horses, an old village pub in Longborough, to the White Hart Royal Hotel, a sixteenth-century inn in Moreton-on-Marsh, the author visits a huge variety of inns and pubs that have made the Cotswolds the delightful area they are today.

978 0 7524 4465 9

The Stroud Valley Illustrated

Stroud has witnessed many changes since the original version of this book was first published over 100 years ago. A fourth reprint, from 1911, was recently discovered in a local resident's collection, and contains many of the advertisements and photographs that were created at the time, giving the modern reader a glimpse into Stroud Valley life all those decades ago. It will certainly be a nostalgic read for those who have lived in the area for many years and members of local historical societies, and a fascinating insight for those visiting or new to the Five Valleys.

978 0 7524 4817 6

Visit our website and discover thousands of other History Press books.
www.thehistorypress.co.uk